An Analysis of

Frank Dikötter's

Mao's Great Famine

John Wagner Givens

Routledge
Taylor & Francis Group

LONDON AND NEW YORK

Published by Macat International Ltd
24:13 Coda Centre, 189 Munster Road, London SW6 6AW.

Distributed exclusively by Routledge
4 Park Square, Milton Park, Abingdon, Oxon OX14 4RN
605 Third Avenue, New York, NY 10017

Routledge is an imprint of the Taylor & Francis Group, an informa business

www.macat.com
info@macat.com

Cataloguing in Publication Data
A catalogue record for this book is available from the British Library.
Library of Congress Cataloguing-in-Publication Data is available upon request.
Cover illustration: Etienne Gilfillan

ISBN 978-1-912302-50-5 (hardback)
ISBN 978-1-912128-04-4 (paperback)
ISBN 978-1-912281-38-1 (e-book)

Notice
The information in this book is designed to orientate readers of the work under analysis,
to elucidate and contextualise its key ideas and themes, and to aid in the development
of critical thinking skills. It is not meant to be used, nor should it be used, as a
substitute for original thinking or in place of original writing or research. References and
notes are provided for informational purposes and their presence does not constitute
endorsement of the information or opinions therein. This book is presented solely for
educational purposes. It is sold on the understanding that the publisher is not engaged
to provide any scholarly advice. The publisher has made every effort to ensure that
this book is accurate and up-to-date, but makes no warranties or representations with
regard to the completeness or reliability of the information it contains. The information
and the opinions provided herein are not guaranteed or warranted to produce particular
results and may not be suitable for students of every ability. The publisher shall not be
liable for any loss, damage or disruption arising from any errors or omissions, or from
the use of this book, including, but not limited to, special, incidental, consequential or
other damages caused, or alleged to have been caused, directly or indirectly, by the
information contained within.

CONTENTS

THE MACAT LIBRARY

The Macat Library is a series of unique academic explorations of seminal works in the humanities and social sciences – books and papers that have had a significant and widely recognised impact on their disciplines. It has been created to serve as much more than just a summary of what lies between the covers of a great book. It illuminates and explores the influences on, ideas of, and impact of that book. Our goal is to offer a learning resource that encourages critical thinking and fosters a better, deeper understanding of important ideas.

Each publication is divided into three Sections: Influences, Ideas, and Impact. Each Section has four Modules. These explore every important facet of the work, and the responses to it.

This Section-Module structure makes a Macat Library book easy to use, but it has another important feature. Because each Macat book is written to the same format, it is possible (and encouraged!) to cross-reference multiple Macat books along the same lines of inquiry or research. This allows the reader to open up interesting interdisciplinary pathways.

To further aid your reading, lists of glossary terms and people mentioned are included at the end of this book (these are indicated by an asterisk [*] throughout) – as well as a list of works cited.

Macat has worked with the University of Cambridge to identify the elements of critical thinking and understand the ways in which six different skills combine to enable effective thinking.
Three allow us to fully understand a problem; three more give us the tools to solve it. Together, these six skills make up the **PACIER** model of critical thinking. They are:

ANALYSIS – understanding how an argument is built
EVALUATION – exploring the strengths and weaknesses of an argument
INTERPRETATION – understanding issues of meaning

CREATIVE THINKING – coming up with new ideas and fresh connections
PROBLEM-SOLVING – producing strong solutions
REASONING – creating strong arguments

To find out more, visit **WWW.MACAT.COM.**

CRITICAL THINKING AND *MAO'S GREAT FAMINE*

Primary critical thinking skill: REASONING
Secondary critical thinking skill: PROBLEM-SOLVING

The power of Frank Dikötter's ground-breaking work on the disaster that followed China's attempted 'Great Leap Forward' lies not in the detail of his evidence (though that shows that Mao's fumbled attempt at rapid industrialization probably cost 45 million Chinese lives). It stems from the exceptional reasoning skills that allowed Dikötter to turn years of researching in obscure Chinese archives into a compelling narrative of disaster, and above all to link two subjects that had been treated as distinct by most of his predecessors: the extent of the crisis in the countryside, and the actions (hence the responsibility) of the senior Chinese leadership.

In Dikötter's view, ultimate responsibility for the catastrophe lies at the door of Mao Zedong himself; the Chairman conceived and ordered the policies that led to the famine, and he did nothing to reverse them or limit the damage that was being wrought when evidence for their disastrous impact reached him. Dikötter's ability to persuade his readers of the fundamental truth of these arguments – despite his admission that his access to sources was necessarily limited and incomplete – together with the clear structure of his presentation combine to produce a work that has had enormous influence on perceptions of Mao and of the Great Leap Forward itself.

ABOUT THE AUTHOR OF THE ORIGINAL WORK

Historian **Frank Dikötter** was born in 1961 in Kerensheide in the Netherlands and took his first degree in history and Russian at the University of Geneva in Switzerland. From there, he won a scholarship to study in China and explored the country as it emerged from the Maoist era. Dikötter earned his doctorate from the School of Oriental and African Studies in London in 1990, and became professor of the modern history of China there. He has been chair of humanities at the University of Hong Kong since 2006. His 2010 work Mao's Great Famine is based on information unearthed in official Communist archives that are usually closed to researchers.

ABOUT THE AUTHOR OF THE ANALYSIS

Dr John Wagner Givens holds a DPhil in politics from the University of Oxford. He is currently an Asian Studies Center Associate and adjunct professor at the University of Pittsburgh, having previously held positions as a post-Doctoral Research Associate at the Center for Asian Democracy at the University of Louisville, as Associate Lecturer at the University of the West of England, and as a Visiting Scholar at Nankai University in Tianjin.

Dr Wagner's research interests span a range of topics including law, foreign policy, and political economy, but he specializes in ostensibly liberal institutions in nondemocratic regimes. He is currently working on a book manuscript on lawyers that sue the Chinese state.

ABOUT MACAT

GREAT WORKS FOR CRITICAL THINKING

Macat is focused on making the ideas of the world's great thinkers accessible and comprehensible to everybody, everywhere, in ways that promote the development of enhanced critical thinking skills.

It works with leading academics from the world's top universities to produce new analyses that focus on the ideas and the impact of the most influential works ever written across a wide variety of academic disciplines. Each of the works that sit at the heart of its growing library is an enduring example of great thinking. But by setting them in context – and looking at the influences that shaped their authors, as well as the responses they provoked – Macat encourages readers to look at these classics and game-changers with fresh eyes. Readers learn to think, engage and challenge their ideas, rather than simply accepting them.

'Macat offers an amazing first-of-its-kind tool for interdisciplinary learning and research. Its focus on works that transformed their disciplines and its rigorous approach, drawing on the world's leading experts and educational institutions, opens up a world-class education to anyone.'

Andreas Schleicher
Director for Education and Skills, Organisation for Economic Co-operation and Development

'Macat is taking on some of the major challenges in university education ... They have drawn together a strong team of active academics who are producing teaching materials that are novel in the breadth of their approach.'

Prof Lord Broers,
former Vice-Chancellor of the University of Cambridge

'The Macat vision is exceptionally exciting. It focuses upon new modes of learning which analyse and explain seminal texts which have profoundly influenced world thinking and so social and economic development. It promotes the kind of critical thinking which is essential for any society and economy. This is the learning of the future.'

Rt Hon Charles Clarke, former UK Secretary of State for Education

'The Macat analyses provide immediate access to the critical conversation surrounding the books that have shaped their respective discipline, which will make them an invaluable resource to all of those, students and teachers, working in the field.'

Professor William Tronzo, University of California at San Diego

WAYS IN TO THE TEXT

KEY POINTS

- Born in 1961, Frank Dikötter is a Dutch historian who specializes in Chinese history at the University of Hong Kong.

- He examines in extraordinary detail the famine caused by the Great Leap Forward* of 1958 to 1961—the Chinese Communist Party's* campaign to jumpstart Chinese industry—showing it to be perhaps the greatest man-made catastrophe in human history.

- *Mao's Great Famine* is the result of four years of research in archives across China and is an unflinching account of how this episode in Chinese history was far worse than previously thought.

Who Was *Frank Dikötter?*

Frank Dikötter, the author of *Mao's Great Famine: The History of China's Most Devastating Catastrophe* (2010), is a well-known scholar of Chinese history who has written ten books and speaks six languages. His early work tended to focus on difficult topics such as drugs, crime, sex, race, and marginalized populations in China. He is best known as a critic of the Chinese Communist Party, the party ruling the nation since 1949, writing a trilogy of histories that cast an unflattering light on the party's early years. The best known of these is *Mao's Great Famine*.

Born in 1961 in Kerensheide in the Netherlands, Frank Dikötter did his undergraduate work at the University of Geneva in Switzerland. There, he was a double major in history and Russian. Dikötter was "attracted to the Soviet Union* by a love of [the Russian author] Dostoyevsky and the allure of the unknown."[1] The Soviet Union was a federation of countries in Eastern Europe and Asia, founded on communist* principles, which collapsed in 1991. After studying for a summer in the city of Leningrad (the second largest city in Russia, today renamed St. Petersburg), he received a scholarship to study in China and spent two years studying and exploring there. This gave him a glimpse of a China that was just beginning to emerge from the Maoist* era (when the country was led by Mao Zedong,* chairman of the Communist Party of China from 1949 until his death in 1976).

Dikötter went on to earn his doctorate from the School of Oriental and African Studies (SOAS) in London in 1990. Conducting research for his doctorate in 1988 and 1989, he happened to be present in Beijing during the lead-up to the Tiananmen Square massacre* that ended student-led demonstrations for democratic reform. He left the city for southern China before the violence broke out.

After graduating he remained at SOAS for nearly 10 years, first as a British Academy Postdoctoral Fellow and Wellcome Research Fellow, then, from 2002, as professor of the modern history of China. Since 2006, Dikötter has held the post of professor of humanities at the University of Hong Kong.[2]

What Does *Mao's Great Famine* Say?

Mao's Great Famine is a revisionist* history (that is, it challenges the orthodox historical interpretations) of the Great Leap Forward—Mao's attempt to speed up China's industrialization. The Great Leap Forward, a significant event of the twentieth century, created the conditions for the Great Chinese Famine;* Dikötter casts the entire episode in a far more dire light than that described by previous scholars and politicians. The established view had been that the Great Chinese Famine was essentially an accident, the product of misguided agricultural and economic policies combined with bad weather.[3]

Dikötter presents compelling evidence of the incredible damage wrought by the Great Leap Forward and the Great Chinese Famine on a number of fronts.

- The Great Leap Forward contributed massively to the degradation of China's environment.
- As much as 40 percent of the nation's housing was destroyed.
- The extreme circumstance of the famine sometimes forced people to do terrible things to neighbors, friends, and family to survive.
- While most deaths came from starvation, around "6 to 8 per cent of the victims were tortured to death or summarily killed."[4]
- Many people also died from being selectively deprived of food for political reasons or because they were too old and sick to work.

Central to *Mao's Great Famine* is Mao Zedong himself. From 1949, when the Chinese Communist Party (CCP) won the Chinese Civil War* and gained sole control over mainland China, until his death in 1976, Mao was the most important leader in the country. For Dikötter, Mao was responsible for the Great Chinese Famine not only because he was China's leader during this period, but also because he "was the key architect of the Great Leap Forward, and thus bears the main responsibility for the catastrophe that followed."[5]

Dikötter shows how Mao and the CCP were to blame in a number of ways, demonstrating that at the same time as hundreds of millions of Chinese people were starving, China was exporting grain and providing aid to foreign countries. He argues that Mao and other top leaders were aware of the problems in the rural areas but ordered villages to increase the amount of grain they were providing to the party. Dikötter provides quotes from top Chinese leaders who appear callously unconcerned with the widespread death that occurred.

In the broadest sense, *Mao's Great Famine* extends beyond the bounds of China. It tells us something important about the relationship between the state and society, and shows that contemporary debates about the size of government are short-sighted, by demonstrating that the quality and *nature* of state involvement can be more relevant than the *level* of state involvement. In the Great Leap Forward, the state did not cause stagnation through overregulation, but rather ripped up the most basic foundations of Chinese society. The Great Leap Forward and the Great Chinese Famine were among history's greatest disasters because of the unresponsive, dogmatic, capricious and overzealous nature of government involvement.

Why Does *Mao's Great Famine* Matter?

The People's Republic of China is one of the most important political, strategic, and economic players in the world. It may be the world's next superpower. Yet it is still governed by the Chinese Communist Party (CCP). This is the same CCP that created the Great Leap Forward and the famine that followed; Dikötter holds it responsible for the deaths of 45 million people.

That single statistic—the number of premature deaths for the years 1958 to 1962—is the easiest way to understand the human cost of the Great Leap Forward and the Great Chinese Famine. Previous estimates generally ranged from 15 million, based on official Chinese statistics, to scholarly calculations of around 30 million.[6] While these are already staggering numbers, Dikötter argues that the true figure must be at least 45 million—and possibly much greater. By describing how people lost their lives in dozens of separate incidents and places, and scaling the figures to the size of the nation, Dikötter adds, methodically and persuasively, another 15 to 30 million to the accepted death toll.

Chen Yizi,* a senior party official who helped compile a massive report on the Maoist era but fled China after the Tiananmen Square massacre, agreed with this number.[7] While previous understandings of the Great Chinese Famine saw it as less of a catastrophe, Dikötter places it on a par with tragedies such as the Cambodian Genocide* (1975–9), which saw as many as three million murdered, the Soviet famine of 1932–3,* in the course of which agricultural reforms led to the deaths of millions by starvation, and even the Holocaust* of World War II,* during which some 11 million people—some 6 million of whom were Jewish—were murdered.

Since Mao, several generations of leaders have come and gone and the CCP's policies have changed almost entirely. Still, the party traces its roots back to the fight against Japanese occupation during World War II. It also looks back to its victory in the Chinese Civil War—a conflict fought between the CCP and the nationalist Kuomintang (KMT)* to decide the ideological and economic nature of China's government. These key events in party history link the CCP to Mao and his generation of leaders, including Deng Xiaoping,* who set the party on its current path after the death of Mao. The CCP has managed to stay in power partly through airbrushing or ignoring the mistakes of the Mao era.

Since Mao's death, the CCP has claimed that Chairman Mao was 70 percent right and 30 percent wrong.[8] *Mao's Great Famine* forces an observant reader to drastically reevaluate these percentages. It also compels us to ask if Mao and his colleagues should join the ranks of history's most infamous despots and mass murderers. As this view spreads, it could force China's current leaders to reevaluate Mao's whole generation and the first three decades of the CCP's rule. It could even undermine the legitimacy of the CCP as it exists today.

NOTES

1 Patrick Brzeski, "Catching up with the Past," *South China Morning Post*, September 4, 2011. http://www.frankdikotter.com/interviews/patrick-brzeski. html, accessed October 21, 2015.

2 Frank Dikötter, "Frank Dikötter's Professional Website." http://www. frankdikotter.com/, accessed October 22, 2015.

3 Matt Schiavenza, "Interview: Frank Dikötter, Author of Mao's Great Famine [UPDATED]," *Asia Society*. http://asiasociety.org/blog/asia/interview-frank-dik%C3%B6tter-author-maos-great-famine-updated, accessed October 30, 2015.

4 Frank Dikötter, *Mao's Great Famine: The History of China's Most Devastating Catastrophe, 1958–62* (London: Bloomsbury, 2010), xi.

5 Dikötter, *Mao's Great Famine,* xiii.

6 Justin Yifu Lin and Dennis Tao Yang, "On the Causes of China's Agricultural Crisis and the Great Leap Famine," *China Economic Review*, 9, no. 2 (1998), China's Great Famine: 125–40, doi:10.1016/S1043-951X(99)80010-8.

7 Dikötter, *Mao's Great Famine*, 323–32.

8 "Chinese Reopen Debate Over Mao's Legacy," *NPR.org*. http://www.npr. org/2011/06/22/137231508/chinese-reopen-debate-over-chairman-maos-legacy, accessed October 23, 2015.

SECTION 1
INFLUENCES

MODULE 1
THE AUTHOR AND THE
HISTORICAL CONTEXT

KEY POINTS

- *Mao's Great Famine* is a groundbreaking history of one the most important but least understood events of the twentieth century.

- Growing up in Europe made Frank Dikötter keenly aware of both the legacy of the Holocaust* (the mass murder of millions of European Jews, and others, in Europe during World War II)* and the reality of the Cold War* (a period of military and diplomatic tension between the United States and the communist* Soviet Union,* and their respective allies, in the decades following World War II).

- As the power of China and the Chinese Communist Party* (CCP) grows, it is increasingly important to understand its recent history.

Why Read this Text?

Mao's Great Famine: The History of China's Most Devastating Catastrophe (2010) by Frank Dikötter is a groundbreaking work on the Great Leap Forward* (the attempt, beginning in 1958, to greatly increase China's industrial output) and the Great Chinese Famine* of 1958 to 1961 that followed. The book lays bare one of the greatest man-made disasters in human history, which caused at least 45 million deaths; according to Dikötter, only World War II (1939–45) had a bigger bodycount. Yet, the famine is generally less known than the Nazi* genocide* during the Holocaust in World War II (the Nazis were the extreme right-wing governing party of Germany), the Soviet leader Joseph Stalin's* purges*

> **❝** I suppose it was a deep fear of ignorance—both of the big events of the past and the world as it is. **❞**
>
> Frank Dikötter, in Patrick Brzeski, "Catching up with the Past," *South China Morning Post*

during the 1930s (a violent exercise in political repression), the Cambodian Genocide* in the 1970s in which three million were killed, or the Armenian Genocide* of 1915 that occurred in what is today Turkey, and saw the deaths of as many as one and a half million ethnic Armenians.

The case for holding the Chinese leadership responsible for the famine is less clear-cut than with these other great calamities of the twentieth century. Even the most damning critics of the then-Chinese leader Mao Zedong* do not say the Great Leap Forward was intentionally designed to cause mass starvation and devastation. Quite the opposite: it was intended to immensely improve the Chinese economy and therefore the living conditions of ordinary people. This makes the question of how much blame top leaders deserve very complicated and Dikötter devotes much of the book to providing an answer.

The Great Chinese Famine is less well known partly because there are very few major histories of the event, on account of the difficulties of gaining access to source material. Whereas World War II and the Holocaust are the subject of countless books, the Great Chinese Famine is covered by only a handful. Of these, *Mao's Great Famine* stands out for being both rigorous and readable. Dikötter was able to gain an unprecedented level of access to primary sources, such as government records and reports, in Chinese regional archives. That this book is the best account of one of the greatest disasters in human history makes it well worth reading. That this disaster was created by a political party not only still in existence, but with an influence that continues to increase dramatically, makes it a critically important text.

In a more general sense, the book also tells us a great deal about relationships between state and society, especially how they can go horribly wrong. It also gives us significant insight not only into the depths of human suffering, but into the appalling things ordinary people are capable of when faced with such suffering.

Author's Life

Frank Dikötter was born in 1961 in Kerensheide in the southern Dutch province of Limburg. Raised in the Netherlands, he went to Switzerland to attend university, graduating with a double major in history and Russian from the University of Geneva.

As an undergraduate, Dikötter spent a summer in Leningrad (a city now known by its previous name, St. Petersburg), to see what it was like on the other side in the Cold War, but decided "Russians aren't all that different from Europeans. Then a teacher suggested that I could easily get another scholarship to China, because no one else wanted to go."[1]

Dikötter spent two years studying in and travelling all over China. He later returned to Beijing while studying for his doctorate in 1988 and 1989. While there, he saw the tanks roll into Beijing and witnessed the start of the stand-off between pro-democracy protesters and the military that would end in the Tiananmen Square massacre.* Dikötter, however, left Beijing before the beginning of the bloodshed.[2] It seems likely that this experience helped shape his critical view of the CCP. Yet this alone cannot explain why he chose to make Mao and the Mao era the target of his criticism.

Dikötter returned to Europe to finish his doctorate at the School of Oriental and African Studies in London in 1990. He remained at SOAS for more than a decade, first as a research fellow and then as a professor of modern Chinese history. In 2006, he moved to Hong Kong to accept the position of chair professor of humanities at the University of Hong Kong.

Dikötter's books tend to focus on marginal populations and taboo topics in China. These include race, sex, drugs, and prison.

Author's Background

Frank Dikötter grew up in Europe in the 1960s and 1970s and when he read about the Holocaust as a schoolboy he was shocked to realize that the atrocities took place in Europe (including the Netherlands) during his father's lifetime. That such a calamity had happened so close to his family without him knowing about it seems to have had a substantial impact on Dikötter; it perhaps explains his need to uncover another of the twentieth century's great but lesser-known horrors, the Great Chinese Famine.

Growing up in Europe when he did also meant Dikötter was influenced by the Cold War,* the period of military tension between the Russian-led Soviet Union and America from 1945 to 1991. "The Cold War was still going strong at that time [the early 1980s]," he explains. "I wanted to know what it was actually like on the other side."[3] This helps explain why Dikötter gravitated toward Russia and then eventually China. Curious about the unknown, it seems he wanted to understand the realities of the communist world on the other side of the Iron Curtain*—the name for the militarized border between the democratic West and the authoritarian East ("authoritarian" here describing the nature of Soviet society, in which the government authority played an intrusive role in the citizens' lives).

In *Mao's Great Famine* Dikötter's desire to examine countries with vastly different cultures and political systems came together with his need to understand and expose great human tragedies.

NOTES

1   Patrick Brzeski, "Catching up with the Past," *South China Morning Post*, September 4, 2011, accessed October 21, 2015, http://www.frankdikotter. com/interviews/patrick-brzeski.html., accessed October 21, 2015.

2   Brzeski, "Catching up with the Past."

3   Brzeski, "Catching up with the Past."

MODULE 2
ACADEMIC CONTEXT

KEY POINTS

- Revisionist* history is aimed at revising our understanding of particular eras, events, and figures from the past.

- A recent trend in history and political science is to show that supposedly powerless people fought back against repression, often in minor but important ways (a concept known as "weapons of the weak"*).

- Dikötter challenges the conventional understanding of the entire era of the Chinese revolutionary leader Mao Zedong.*

The Work In Its Context

Mao's Great Famine: The History of China's Most Devastating Catastrophe by Frank Dikötter is a work of revisionist history. A crucial element of good historical revisionism is that it often comes from finding or gaining access to new sources, for example when lost documents are found or government papers are declassified. In the case of *Mao's Great Famine*, Dikötter managed to see previously unavailable documents in several regional archives throughout China during a period of political openness in the lead-up to the 2008 Beijing Olympics.

Another key aspect of historical revisionism is that it involves taking a fresh look at the motivations and decisions made by the people involved in the events in question. New sources can reveal previously unknown circumstances that throw a whole new light on the actions of certain leaders. A case in point is when the English military historian Gary Sheffield* and his colleagues showed how previously overlooked problems with military communications hampered the effectiveness of British generals, who had previously

> **66** Revolution is not a dinner party. **99**
>
> Mao Zedong, *The Little Red Book*

been seen as simply incompetent.[1] This type of revisionism plays an important part in *Mao's Great Famine* too. Dikötter takes another look at the actions of China's top leaders, especially Mao, and shows that they knew far more than previously thought about the catastrophic consequences of the Great Leap Forward* of 1958—the attempt to transform China's society and economy by greatly increasing industrial output in the space of a few years.

Overview of the Field

The most important trend in revisionism is the effort to understand the views of marginalized groups and people. Revisionist histories tend to investigate a long list of "subjects that historians had previously slighted," such as "Indian history, black history, women's history, family history."[2] This is sometimes known as "social history"*—a historical account taking special account of the experiences of ordinary people. Perhaps the best-known example is the political scientist Howard Zinn's* *A People's History of the United States*, which actually summarizes a lot of revisionist American history.[3] *Mao's Great Famine* only partially falls into this category. The book does have chapters devoted to vulnerable groups such as children, women, and the elderly. Dikötter, however, shows that the Great Leap Forward and the Great Chinese Famine* had a tremendous impact on nearly everyone living in China.

At its most basic, historical revisionism simply means challenging and reassessing the status quo. Taking such a broad view, *Mao's Great Famine* can be seen as a revision of previous work on the Mao era in two major ways.

First, traditional histories tend to focus on high-ranking leaders and political conflicts. Books that concentrate on top Chinese

Communist Party* (CCP) leaders are important for helping us to understand why and how the Great Leap Forward and then the Great Chinese Famine came about.[4] Dikötter relies on these for the first two parts of his book to explain the political context for the Great Chinese Famine. Established histories emphasize the political logic of the Great Leap Forward, but pay little attention to the havoc on the ground. The best-known example of such a work is *The Origins of the Cultural Revolution, Volume 2: The Great Leap Forward, 1958–1960* by the British historian Roderick MacFarquhar.*[5]

Second, some previous assessments of the Great Chinese Famine relied on high-level official statistics to assess the damage done by mass starvation. In Dikötter's words, "researchers so far have had to extrapolate from official population statistics, including the census figures of 1953, 1964, and 1982. Their estimates range from 15 to 32 million excess deaths."[6] By using more detailed, diverse, and lower-level sources, Dikötter makes a convincing case that these tended to vastly underestimate the death and destruction brought on by the Great Leap Forward and the Great Chinese Famine. Dikötter explains that "the public security reports compiled at the time, as well as the voluminous secret reports collated by party committees in the last months of the Great Leap Forward, show how inadequate these calculations are, pointing instead at a catastrophe of a much greater magnitude: this book shows that at least 45 million people died unnecessarily between 1958 and 1962."[7]

Academic Influences

Mao's Great Famine uses a great deal of factual evidence, mostly from primary sources. For this reason it does not draw heavily on other academic work, although it is in the tradition of history writing about famine, mass death, and genocide.*

Dikötter's work does, though, draw on studies of "weapons of the weak"—a term originated by the American political scientist James Scott.* [8] In his extensive studies of peasants and slave societies, Scott identified how even the least powerful individuals resist domination by actions that include stealing small amounts of food, running away from military service, working slowly, and poaching animals on land belonging to lords or masters. In Scott's view, these small acts of resistance build up over time and can topple a social, economic, or political system.[9]

Dikötter identifies many of these small acts of resistance during the Great Chinese Famine. For example, farmers ate unripe grain directly from the fields or hid grain from the state.[10] There were also much more aggressive actions, such as setting fire to state granaries.[11]

Dikötter, however, does not agree with Scott because his examples from the famine contradict Scott in two ways. Dikötter points out that many acts of "resistance" were not aimed at, or did not hurt, the state. They just ended up hurting other oppressed people—the farmer who ate grain in the fields, for example, deprived others in his village from eating that grain when it was ripe. Also, these acts were so widespread that if they had indeed been a meaningful form of resistance they would have brought down the CCP.

NOTES

1   Gary Sheffield, "The Western Front: Lions Led by Donkeys?" BBC.com. http://www.bbc.co.uk/history/worldwars/wwone/lions_donkeys_01.shtml, accessed January21, 2016.

2   Forest McDonald. *Recovering the Past: A Historian's Memoir* (Lawrence: University Press of Kansas, 2004), 114.

3   Michael Kammen. "How the Other Half Lived." *Washington Post Book World*, March 23, 1980, 7.

4   Roderick MacFarquhar, *The Origins of the Cultural Revolution, Volume 2* (London: Columbia University Press, 1983); Alfred L. Chan, *Mao's Crusade : Politics and Policy Implementation in China's Great Leap Forward* (Oxford: Oxford University Press, 2001); David Bachman, *Bureaucracy, Economy, and Leadership in China: The Institutional Origins of the Great Leap Forward* (Cambridge: Cambridge University Press, 2006); Li Zhisui, *The Private Life of Chairman Mao* (New York: Random House, 2011).

5   MacFarquhar, *The Origins of the Cultural Revolution, Volume 2.*

6   Frank Dikötter, *Mao's Great Famine: The History of China's Most Devastating Catastrophe, 1958–62* (London: Bloomsbury, 2010), ii.

7   Dikötter, *Mao's Great Famine*, ii.

8   Dikötter, *Mao's Great Famine*, xv, 209.

9   James C. Scott, "Weapons of the Weak: Everyday Forms of Peasant Resistance" (New Haven, CT: Yale University Press, 1985).

10 Dikötter, *Mao's Great Famine*, 210, 211.

11 Dikötter, *Mao's Great Famine*, 135.w

MODULE 3
THE PROBLEM

KEY POINTS

- *Mao's Great Famine* tackles two vital questions—what was the true impact of the Great Leap Forward* and the Great Chinese Famine,* and how much blame do China's top leaders deserve for what happened?

- Many earlier history books talked about the political fights among the people at the top, but not about the harsh realities for the mass of ordinary people and how far China's leaders understood those realities.

- Dikötter aims to put this right by documenting the impact of the famine in painstaking detail and showing that leaders knew about the disastrous results of the Great Leap Forward from a very early stage.

Core Question

In *Mao's Great Famine: The History of China's Most Devastating Catastrophe* Frank Dikötter asks two of the most basic and important questions about the Great Leap Forward and the Great Chinese Famine: How bad was it? And who was responsible?

These questions are more difficult to answer in this case than they are for other great tragedies of the twentieth century such as the Holocaust* of World War II,* the Cambodian Genocide* of 1975–9, and the Armenian Genocide* of 1915. In part, this is because the Chinese Communist Party* (CCP), the party of government since 1949, is still in power. This makes access to records in China much more difficult, especially when they refer to the Communist leadership. All the political parties and governments that held sway over other horrors from history (the Communist Party* of the Soviet Union,*

> **❝** Democide—that is, genocide and mass murder—is the most serious threat to humankind in our century ... estimates of democide are very uncertain and often propagandistic. **❞**
>
> Rudolph J. Rummel, "Power, Genocide and Mass Murder"

the communist* Khmer Rouge* in Cambodia, the extreme right-wing Nazi* party in Germany, and the empire of the Ottoman* dynasty in what is today Turkey) have long since left power.

Mao Zedong* was undeniably the most powerful political force in China, and the Great Leap Forward was his idea. The question of blame therefore tends to revolve around how far Mao himself can be held responsible for the disastrous effects of the policy.

The Participants

In the debate about the Great Leap Forward and the Great Chinese Famine, people fall into two categories—those interested primarily in the events, and those who are more concerned with Mao Zedong and his legacy.

Besides *Mao's Great Famine* there are only two other major English-language books in the first category, Jasper Becker's* *Hungry Ghosts* (1996) and the Chinese journalist Yang Jisheng's* *Tombstone: The Great Chinese Famine* (2008). Becker approaches Mao, the Great Leap Forward, and the Great Chinese Famine as a journalist, and offers a view as negative and angry as Dikötter's.[1] His account is not, however, as meticulously detailed and sourced as Dikötter's.[2] Meanwhile *Tombstone*, according to one review, is "a condensed, yet magisterial 600-page edition of a densely detailed, two-volume Chinese-language account by Yang Jisheng [who] lacks Mr. Dikötter's narrative skills," and readers may find it "heavy going at times."[3]

There are far more works that fall into the second category, addressing Mao's legacy more generally. The most important was written by Mao's doctor and confidant, Li Zhisui.* In *The Private Life of Chairman Mao: The Memoirs of Mao's Personal Physician* (1994), Zhisui presents Mao as complicated, brilliant, and insightful but ultimately deeply flawed. His faults seem to outweigh his virtues. In *Mao: The Unknown Story* (2005), the Chinese British writer Jung Chang* and her collaborator Jon Halliday* offer a scathing account of Mao, summed up by one reviewer as "a brutal, sadistic power-monger lacking in vision or ideals, comfort-loving and often lazy, riding the revolution to power to satisfy a lust for torture and sex."[4] Most scholars find Chang and Halliday's account too extreme and difficult to verify to be completely believable.

These revealing biographies of Mao help explain his role at the center of the greatest famine in human history. It is possible to see a man so confident in his own abilities that he believed the unrealistic reports about the success of the Great Leap Forward, and sufficiently self-deluded or callous to ignore mounting evidence of the incredible hardships his policies caused. Dikötter relies heavily on Li's account of Mao and frequently points to *The Private Life of Chairman Mao* as a guide to the kind of person who could have created the Great Chinese Famine.

The Contemporary Debate

In mainstream accounts of Chinese history, the Great Leap Forward was seen as a highly flawed and misguided attempt to advance China's development. Its disastrous results were blamed on naïvety, incompetence, and ignorance as "tens of millions of people died unnecessarily 'as a result of terrible decisions, crop failures and food shortages.'"[5] In such accounts, Mao and other leaders are seen as committing grave mistakes, not as causing, ignoring, or even exacerbating one of the greatest calamities in human history.

Mao's Great Famine challenges this conventional wisdom by

showing that Mao and others in power were neither ignorant of the suffering they had caused nor powerless to stop it. Dikötter found hundreds of documents that should have alerted China's leaders to the disastrous consequences of their policies. Frightened local leaders covered up some of these damning reports, but many were definitely seen by Mao and others in the government. China carried on sending grain and cash abroad even after the scale of the famine was known.

Mao's Great Famine forces us to look again at books that cast Mao and other Chinese leaders in a less negative light. The CCP united and brought peace to China after decades of war. It helped bring literacy to hundreds of millions of people. It helped tear down traditional prejudices about women. These accomplishments, however, pale in comparison to the horrors described in Dikötter's book.

When it comes to the debate over the level of state involvement in day-to-day life (especially in rural areas) in the Mao era, Dikötter's contribution is small but important. He brings subtlety to an overly simplistic debate by adding the detail through facts and examples. *Mao's Great Famine* argues that Mao's policies obviously had a huge impact even in remote rural areas, but the government had almost no control over how those policies were implemented, and faced constant resistance.

NOTES

1   Jasper Becker, *Hungry Ghosts: Mao's Secret Famine* (New York: Macmillan, 1998).

2   Lucien Bianco, "Frank Dikötter, Mao's Great Famine, The History of China's Most Devastating Catastrophe, 1958–62," trans. N. Jayaram, *China Perspectives*, no. 2011/2 (July 30, 2011): 74–5.

3   Michael Fathers, "A Most Secret Tragedy," *Wall Street Journal*, October 26, 2012, Life and Style section. http://www.wsj.com/articles/SB100008723963 90444180004578015170039623486, accessed January 22, 2016.

4   Andrew Nathan, "Jade and Plastic," *London Review of Books*, November 17, 2005, 10.

5   Matt Schiavenza, "Interview: Frank Dikötter, Author of Mao's Great Famine [UPDATED]," *Asia Society*. http://asiasociety.org/blog/asia/interview-frank-dik%C3%B6tter-author-maos-great-famine-updated, accessed October 30, 2015.

MODULE 4
THE AUTHOR'S CONTRIBUTION

KEY POINTS

- Frank Dikötter's aim in *Mao's Great Famine* is to reveal the grim realities of one the most momentous and little-discussed events of the twentieth century: the Great Chinese Famine.*

- He builds on existing scholarship that tended to study political conflict and government infighting in Mao's China, but moves beyond to examine the true scope of the famine.

- While previous work gave us a glimpse of the horrors of the famine, Dikötter's excellent scholarship brings us a highly detailed and well-supported account of the episode.

Author's Aims

Frank Dikötter wrote *Mao's Great Famine: The History of China's Most Devastating Catastrophe* as a social history* of the Great Leap Forward,* China's attempt to speed up industrialization from 1958. Social history has become an increasingly popular approach over the last 50 years. Before *Mao's Great Famine*, the difficulty of accessing original sources such as official Chinese records meant nobody had been able to write a similarly comprehensive account of the period.

Dikötter also had two more specific aims. He wanted to expose the horrors of the Great Leap Forward and the Great Chinese Famine as much worse than previously thought. And he wanted to put the blame squarely on senior figures in the Chinese Communist Party* (CCP), specifically the supreme leader, Mao Zedong.* Dikötter's figure of 45 million needless deaths is supported by careful documentation of the widespread human suffering of the era. Dikötter

66 The significance of the book thus is by no means confined to the famine. What it chronicles, often in harrowing detail, is the near collapse of a social and economic system on which Mao had staked his prestige. As the catastrophe unfolded, the Chairman lashed out at his critics to maintain his position as the indispensable leader of the party. 99

Frank Dikötter, *Mao's Great Famine: The History of China's Most Devastating Catastrophe*

plainly shows that while the policies of the Great Leap Forward may have sprung from good intentions, they were extremely misguided and poorly thought out.

Specifically, he shows that unrealistically high targets were set for the production of everything from rice to steel. These were intended to be "the key to industrialising a backward countryside without big foreign investment."[1] The failure of these policies became apparent fairly quickly. "Tell-tale signs of famine were gangs of people shuffling along dusty roads begging for food, leaving behind empty villages. [Yet] Li Xiannian, minister of finance, swept these reservations aside and pressed ahead with grain targets."[2] However, Mao was unwilling to admit "the near collapse of a social and economic system on which [he] had staked his prestige. As the catastrophe unfolded, the Chairman lashed out at his critics to maintain his position as the indispensable leader of the party."[3] Instead of fixing the problems it had created, Mao ensured that the CCP doubled down on obviously failing policies, turning a series of policy blunders into one of the greatest catastrophes in human history. Worse, much of this was engineered by Mao simply to keep himself at the top of China's political hierarchy.

Approach

Dikötter's strategy is to back up his arguments with as much historical documentation as possible. His findings are related in the form of a stream of statistics and anecdotes. Dikötter rarely skimps on detail, putting descriptions of the gory aspects of specific incidents above broader historical narratives.

The power of Dikötter's work comes from the strength of his sources. While he is hardly the first historian to use them, he was able to get better access and make better use of the party archives for three reasons. First, he spent four years going through dozens of different archives all over China. Second, he took advantage of a new law relating to archived material.[4] And third, he made full use of the relative openness and goodwill that was evident in the lead-up to the Beijing Olympics in 2008 to get into the archives.

When Dikötter makes assertions about the horrors of the Great Leap Forward and the Great Chinese Famine he backs them up with large numbers of examples and statistics. He discusses at length how elderly people were left to die, how parents sold their children in exchange for food, and how some people resorted to cannibalism. Even for a fairly minor point, Dikötter provides several pages of examples and statistics. For example, he shows how collectivization* (the policy of requiring farmers to pool their land for the state to run) led to a number of incidents of poisoning.[5]

In his review of *Mao's Great Famine*, the Australia-based China scholar Anthony Garnaut* writes that "Dikötter claims his book 'brings together two dimensions of the catastrophe that have so far been studied in isolation', linking 'the corridors of Zhongnanhai' [the compound where China's top leaders live and work] with 'the everyday experiences of ordinary people.'"[6] In other words, Dikötter openly connects Mao and his fellow leaders to the famine. Garnaut continues by saying that "the main technique he uses to achieve this is one of juxtaposition [placing two things together for comparison or contrast]. The words of Mao and other central Party leaders are juxtaposed against things that happened in a certain village at an uncertain time."[7] This technique was necessary because the documents unearthed by Dikötter seldom deal with high-level politics.

Contribution in Context

The contribution made by *Mao's Great Famine* is not limited to the study of modern China, or even to the discipline of history. It also provides valuable insight for fields such as economics, politics, and sociology (the study of the functioning of society, and of social behavior more broadly).

Dikötter's contribution does not lie, however, in the originality of his analysis. Other authors made similar claims about the devastating effect of the Great Leap Forward and the Great Chinese Famine. It is in the detailed and carefully cited historical research that underpins everything in the book, giving weight to his insistence that previous estimates of the death toll were far too low. The debate about the Great Chinese Famine also has implications for the size and scale of other mass deaths where the accepted body count is, effectively, a guess. It is also important in discussing who takes responsibility for wiping out millions of people. The debates about how many lost lives the Soviet* leader Joseph Stalin* was responsible for in the political repression known as "the purges"* of the 1930s face similar issues. Some scholars claim the number of deaths Stalin can be blamed for is no more than 2 million; others calculate it at 4.8 million, while Steven Rosefielde, professor of economics at the University of North Carolina, claims it must be at least 5.2 million and is probably around 10 million.[8]

NOTES

1   Frank Dikötter, *Mao's Great Famine: The History of China's Most Devastating Catastrophe*, 1958–62 (London: Bloomsbury, 2010), 56.

2   Dikötter, *Mao's Great Famine*, 67.

3 Dikötter, *Mao's Great Famine*, 5.

4 Dikötter, *Mao's Great Famine*, 7.

5 Dikötter, *Mao's Great Famine*, 184–90.

6 Anthony Garnaut, "Hard Facts and Half-Truths: The New Archival History of China's Great Famine," *China Information* 27, no. 2 (July 1, 2013): 232, doi:10.1177/0920203X13485390.

7 Garnaut, "Hard Facts and Half-Truths," 232.

8 Steven Rosefielde, "Documented Homicides and Excess Deaths: New Insights into the Scale of Killing in the USSR during the 1930s," *Communist and Post-Communist Studies* 30, no. 3 (September 1997): 321–31, doi:10.1016/S0967-067X(97)00011-1.

SECTION 2
IDEAS

MODULE 5
MAIN IDEAS

KEY POINTS

- *Mao's Great Famine* examines the catastrophic impact of a misguided and overzealous government and the often desperate reactions of ordinary people.

- The policies forced on the population by China's leaders caused the greatest peacetime catastrophe in human history.

- Frank Dikötter sets out his assessment of the disaster caused by the Great Leap Forward* in exceptional and extremely well documented detail.

Key Themes

In *Mao's Great Famine: The History of China's Most Devastating Catastrophe*, Frank Dikötter lays out in detail the realities of the Chinese leader Mao Zedong's* Great Leap Forward and the Great Chinese Famine* it caused. Dikötter's central theme is the incredible arrogance and willful ignorance that near-absolute power seems to have instilled in Mao and his closest colleagues, and the disastrous consequences this had for the Chinese people.

The Great Leap Forward policy was supposed to force the pace of industrialization—the move towards an economy and society founded on industrial production—and the Chinese Communist Party* (CCP) set increasingly high targets for the production of agricultural and industrial goods. Dikötter argues that this was done to feed Mao's ego, to enable him to assert his power over the party, and to compete with the Soviet Union.* In the beginning, these high production targets were merely ambitious. But then, under

> **❝ Between 1958 and 1962, China descended into hell. ❞**
>
> Frank Dikötter, *Mao's Great Famine: The History of China's Most Devastating Catastrophe*

pressure to meet their quotas, lower-ranking officials started inflating their production numbers. Soon "every level [of the party was] feeding false reports and inflated statistics to the next one up."[1] This led Mao to ramp up production targets to dizzying and completely unrealistic heights, while bragging to the Soviets about China's remarkable accomplishment.[2]

Local officials went to extreme lengths to try to meet—or at least look like they were meeting—these unrealistic targets, often with disastrous consequences. Officials higher up the command chain then requisitioned grain based on these inflated numbers, leaving almost nothing for the farmers who produced it. The result was the Great Chinese Famine.

More traditional views of the Great Leap Forward maintain that problems were hidden from Mao, though he did create the political environment that fostered misinformation. Dikötter shows, however, that the failures of the Great Leap Forward and the looming famine were both quite clear by 1959. The problems were visible even to foreign students studying in China.[3] Dikötter demonstrates Mao's blithe response to the famine with a quote from a 1959 meeting: "When there is not enough to eat people starve to death. It is better to let half of the people die so that the other half can eat their fill."[4] However, Anthony Garnaut* disputes the context of this quotation, arguing that "[t]he 'people' whom Mao was willing to let die of starvation turn out to be not people at all, but large-scale industrial projects."[5]

In perhaps the most callous and ill-conceived of the era's policies, China's leadership sent huge amounts of grain and money abroad in the midst of famine at home. Some of these shipments were unnecessarily early payments made on debts to the Soviet Union; some were payment for massive purchases of industrial and military hardware; and others were sent as economic aid or interest-free or low-interest loans, or as free grain simply given to other countries. In the midst of incredible hardship, these policies came from Mao's desire to make China and himself look good and outshine the Soviets.[6] Dikötter argues that Mao staked his reputation on the Great Leap Forward and found it difficult to back down. Rather than try to fix the strategy, Mao threatened and sometimes punished those who tried to speak out against his policies or reveal the truth of the situation.

Exploring The Ideas

Perhaps even more remarkable than the CCP's arrogance in setting unrealistic production targets and its heartlessness in ignoring clear signs of disaster was the extraordinary way the catastrophe played out at grassroots level. Here, Dikötter's detailed research makes its greatest contribution to the story.

In order to help local officials meet increasingly unrealistic production goals, the party leadership promoted poorly thought-out schemes. Dikötter explains how labor was wasted by planting crops too close together, depleting soil and causing crops to rot in the field.[7] Also, the people most capable of productive work were taken away from farming to work on projects that were often useless and sometimes completely counterproductive. The most famous of these were the tens of thousands of "backyard furnaces" built all over rural China. People's homes were "stripped of cooking utensils and agricultural implements to feed the backyard furnaces" only for villagers to be "handed back useless ingots of brittle iron."[8] While the furnaces were intended to produce iron to feed China's young steel industry, huge amounts of effort and fuel were poured into turning useful items into useless iron that was too brittle for steel production.

These schemes also ended up doing incredible damage to China's built and natural environment. "Up to 40 per cent of all housing was turned into rubble, as homes were pulled down to create fertiliser, to build canteens, to relocate villagers, to straighten roads, to make room for a better future or simply to punish their occupants."[9] Forests were chopped down and waterways dammed up with little consideration for the disastrous environmental consequences. In Dikötter's words: "We will never know the full extent of forest coverage lost during the Great Leap Forward, but a prolonged and intense attack on nature claimed up to half of all trees in some provinces."[10]

Language And Expression

Mao's Great Famine is written in a straightforward style. Dikötter prefers to let the shocking facts of the Great Leap Forward and the Great Chinese Famine speak for themselves because he knows his argument risks sounding exaggerated. He prefers to stick to facts, examples, and statistics; the material is so extreme it needs little comment.

As a result, the book tends to be extremely dry. Long passages list example after example and statistic after statistic. At times, this makes the work feel rather long and a little ponderous. Examples draw us back time and time again to obscure parts of rural China. The book is divided into chapters around specific ways of dying (accidents, disease, the Gulag [prison camps], violence, sites of horror, cannibalism), which means the same or similar examples are repeated.

While its overall style does, in this way, take something away from the book's readability it serves the intended purpose of making it feel like a serious history about a topic that could otherwise easily fall prey to exaggeration. It also gives the reader little respite from the relentless horror of the famine.

NOTES

1   Frank Dikötter, *Mao's Great Famine: The History of China's Most Devastating Catastrophe, 1958–62* (London: Bloomsbury, 2010), 219.

2   Dikötter, *Mao's Great Famine*, 42.

3   Dikötter, *Mao's Great Famine*, 213.

4   Dikötter, *Mao's Great Famine*, 86.

5   Anthony Garnaut, "Hard Facts and Half-Truths: The New Archival History of China's Great Famine," *China Information* 27, no. 2 (July 1, 2013): 238, doi:10.1177/0920203X13485390.

6   Dikötter, *Mao's Great Famine*, 111.

7   Dikötter, *Mao's Great Famine*, 39–40, 60-2.

8   Dikötter, *Mao's Great Famine*, 142.

9   Dikötter, *Mao's Great Famine*, XII.

10 Dikötter, *Mao's Great Famine*, XI.

MODULE 6
SECONDARY IDEAS

KEY POINTS

- *Mao's Great Famine* provides invaluable insights for anyone debating the size, role, and quality of government.

- Frank Dikötter gives an unflinching account of how dire situations force ordinary people to do desperate and terrible things to each other in an effort to survive.

- While the Great Chinese Famine* killed millions more people than other catastrophes such as the Holocaust* in World War II,* it is still seen as a tragedy for China rather than for humanity.

Other Ideas

Mao's Great Famine: The History of China's Most Devastating Catastrophe by Frank Dikötter is deliberately written as a book that stays close to the facts. There are two ideas, though, that are notably important to the thrust of the argument even if not mentioned often. The first is that the Great Chinese Famine was the result of a state that pursued ambitious and misguided polices despite being unable to implement them successfully and unwilling to monitor them closely. The second is that, faced with the reality of starvation and worse, ordinary people often turned on each other. Both make the text relevant to times and places beyond China and the twentieth century.

Dikötter argues that Mao Zedong's* government did not stifle China's economy with overregulation—that is, with the burden of intrusive and numerous regulations. Nor was it too small or lacking in the power to govern successfully. The famine was not the result of an economy smothered by a totalitarian state (that is, a state in which every

> ❝ But in the end, when the food ran out, people turned on each other, stealing from other villagers, neighbours or even relatives. Children and the elderly suffered most, for instance when a blind grandmother was robbed of the little rice she had been able to buy ... In the countryside, fierce competition for survival gradually eroded any sense of social cohesion. ❞
>
> Frank Dikötter, *Mao's Great Famine: The History of China's Most Devastating Catastrophe*

aspect of the citizen's life is subject to government control). It was the result of a state that massively overreached its abilities in an effort to implement policies that were at best misguided and that in many cases defied all logic. *Mao's Great Famine* shows that it is not the size of the government that is the issue, but rather its quality and nature. This gives the text relevance in areas such as modern politics in the West.

Dikötter shows that time and again throughout the Great Leap Forward,* ordinary people faced with horrific circumstances were forced into doing horrible things to neighbors, friends, and even family members. An entire chapter is devoted to cannibalism.* While cases were relatively rare, they show how quickly the fabric of society disintegrated and moral qualms vanished. Many famine victims died even when there was enough food. They were starved for political reasons or simply because they were too old, weak, or sick to work. Another "6 to 8 per cent of all the famine victims were directly killed or died as a result of injuries inflicted by cadres [that is, groups of Communist Party activists] and the militia."[1] These troubling revelations link the text to other great tragedies throughout history and even to questions of human nature.

Dikötter argues that when collectivization* destroyed all incentive to work, "violence became a routine tool of control. It was not used occasionally on a few to instil fear in the many, rather it was directed systematically and habitually against anybody seen to dawdle, obstruct or protest, let alone pilfer or steal—a majority of villagers."[2] While this helps explain the incredible cruelty of local officials trying to force extra work out of starving villagers, Dikötter does not offer a clear explanation as to why ordinary people were willing to commit unspeakable acts. These included parents starving, strangling, or drowning children who had become a burden.[3] Instead he provides countless anecdotes and allows readers to draw their own conclusions. Dikötter appears to believe that under extreme enough circumstances many (maybe most) people can be forced into desperate atrocities. He blames Mao and the Chinese Communist Party* (CCP) for creating an environment where so many people were so desperate that such appalling events became commonplace.

Exploring The Ideas

Although supporters of small government like to use *Mao's Great Famine* to support their point of view, a close reading of the book shows that big government is not necessarily an intrusive force that strangles prosperity and liberty. Dikötter points to it being the CCP's overreach (that is, overuse of its power) that showed up its lack of effective governance most profoundly. For example, it was able to force farmers to do close cropping (planting crops very close to each other) and deep plowing—things many farmers knew to be counterproductive or even disastrous.[4] At the same time, party leaders could not even produce accurate estimates of grain production.

Dikötter does not buy into the "weapons of the weak"* thesis either—the idea that the powerless resist with little acts of sabotage and disobedience. He points out that what might be thought of as resistance was just a desperate attempt to survive; these acts were more likely to hurt other desperate people than undermine the state. In Dikötter's words: "To romanticize what were often utterly desperate ways of surviving is to see the world in black and white, when in reality collectivization forced everybody, at one point or another, to make grim moral compromises."[5] This makes *Mao's Great Famine* relevant to countless human tragedies throughout human history. It supports, for example, the Italian author and Auschwitz* survivor Primo Levi's* lament that in the Nazi* death camps "the best had perished and the worst had survived."[6] Auschwitz was a group of camps in Poland in which at least a million people, mostly Jewish, were murdered at the hands of the extreme right-wing Nazi regime in the course of World War II.

Overlooked

Mao's Great Famine is a recent work of scholarship, having only appeared in 2010, so it is too early to claim that any of Dikötter's themes or ideas have been overlooked.

However, it is true to say that judging by its reception to date, the work has not had a great impact beyond the study of China. The book has been cited well over three hundred times, but most of these are in other work about China.

In terms of man-made disasters, only World War II exceeds the death toll of the Great Chinese Famine. The Chinese catastrophe resulted in many more deaths than the Holocaust in wartime Europe. The implications of the Holocaust for the whole world and all humanity have been considered many times, yet the famine tends to be viewed only as an incident in Chinese history, rather than in world or human history. This is partly due to a Eurocentric* viewpoint (seeing world events through European, or, by extension, Western, eyes). It is also the result of events being restricted to one country, mainly in the rural areas, and having taken so long to come to light.

As China's importance in the world continues to grow, perhaps *Mao's Great Famine*'s universal themes of desperation and overzealous and incompetent government will be better recognized.

NOTES

1   Frank Dikötter, *Mao's Great Famine: The History of China's Most Devastating Catastrophe, 1958–62* (London: Bloomsbury, 2010), 296.

2   Dikötter, *Mao's Great Famine*, 290.

3   Dikötter, *Mao's Great Famine*, 250.

4   Dikötter, *Mao's Great Famine*, 39.

5   Dikötter, *Mao's Great Famine*, xv.

6   James Wood, "The Art of Witness," *The New Yorker*, September 28, 2015. http://www.newyorker.com/magazine/2015/09/28/the-art-of-witness, accessed 27 October 2015.

MODULE 7
ACHIEVEMENT

KEY POINTS

- Frank Dikötter achieved his goal of writing the definitive history of the Great Leap Forward* and the Great Chinese Famine.*

- Although several recent books criticize Mao Zedong* and the Chinese Communist Party* (CCP), *Mao's Great Famine* stands out as a particularly fine work, being both scholarly and readable.

- Dikötter's work is based on documents from only a section of the official archives in China; many others remain locked away.

Assessing The Argument

In *Mao's Great Famine: The History of China's Most Devastating Catastrophe* Frank Dikötter provides overwhelming evidence for his arguments. Countless examples drive home the horror of the Great Leap Forward (the attempt to rapidly industrialize China) and the famine that followed. These facts, figures, and stories reveal a determination to leave no doubt in the minds of readers about the scale and awfulness of the events. Above all else, *Mao's Great Famine* is written as a definitive history of one of the twentieth century's most important but least discussed tragedies. Dikötter achieves this goal, providing the best-known work about the CCP policy in the late 1950s and the mass starvation it caused.

As a retelling of history carefully based on documentary evidence, any limitation in sources is a significant limitation in the argument itself. Dikötter readily admits that he was not able to see all of the records. He had especially good access to some local archives in China

❝ Frank Dikötter's work, appearing half a century after the most murderous year (1960), will henceforth be the leading account on the 'Great Famine.' **❞**

Lucien Bianco, "Frank Dikötter, Mao's Great Famine, The History of China's Most Devastating Catastrophe, 1958–62"

during the relatively open period leading up to the Olympics in 2008. These represented only a small section of the local records, though, to say nothing of central archives stored in Beijing. In Dikötter's own words, "truly sensitive material remains out of bounds except to the eyes of the most senior party members. The very fact that this distinction removes from the scrutiny of most historians a large proportion of vital information indicates that this book has been written with relatively 'soft' material."[1]

Dikötter argues that the blame for the Great Chinese Famine rests squarely on the shoulders of Mao and his colleagues. The argument is highly plausible and many readers might agree that China's rulers should have known, and probably did know, about the horrors the Great Leap Forward unleashed. However, Dikötter's sources still do not provide a "smoking gun" that unequivocally connects top leaders to the Great Leap Forward's disastrous outcomes. That will be assessed only when the CCP's central archives are open to historians.

Achievement In Context

As *Mao's Great Famine* was only published in 2010, it is too early to judge the full extent of its influence. Yet the work certainly benefits from having appeared when worldwide interest in China was increasing along with the growth of its economy. Westerners are apprehensive about the rising power of China and many are ready to hear the worst about its recent history and leaders.

More than this, the book appeared before the 2012 English translation of the Chinese journalist Yang Jisheng's* Chinese-language account *Tombstone: The Great Chinese Famine, 1958–1962* of 2008. As both books take similar approaches to the disaster, Dikötter's book might have been less well received if it had come out just a few years later than it did.[2]

Mao's Great Famine emerged during a decade when other damning accounts of Mao and the CCP appeared. It stands out as one of the strongest, thanks largely to the extensive research Dikötter managed to do in archives usually closed to historians. Along with these other works, it forces us to reconsider the history of China's Communist Party.

Limitations

Mao's Great Famine is a meticulously researched work of history. Its main limitation is that it puts concrete facts, examples, and statistics before the broader historical narrative. In other words, Dikötter pays more attention to the details of what happened than he does to painting the bigger picture. This is certainly intentional and may have been the best choice for the sober, scholarly tone he clearly wanted to achieve. Yet it prevents the book from joining the ranks of truly great histories. Such works as the six-volume *History of the Decline and Fall of the Roman Empire* by the British historian Edward Gibbon* (1776),[3] the German American political theorist Hannah Arendt's* *Eichmann in Jerusalem: A Report on the Banality of Evil* (1963),[4] and the British historian Eric Hobsbawm's* trilogy on late-eighteenth- and nineteenth-century European political and economic history (1962, 1975, 1987) all present sweeping stories about the past.

These works spell out theories for exactly how to understand broad sections of history, societies at large, and even human nature; *Mao's Great Famine*, on the other hand, is so full of examples, statistics, and anecdotes and so sparse on narrative and explanation that it reads at times like a list of atrocities and horrors rather than a great work of history. Dikötter simply does not do the work of explaining the larger implications of his research, which is presented as page after page of human suffering.

NOTES

1   Frank Dikötter, *Mao's Great Famine: The History of China's Most Devastating Catastrophe, 1958–62* (London: Bloomsbury, 2010), 341.

2   Rana Mitter, "*Tombstone: The Untold Story of Mao's Great Famine* by Yang Jisheng – Review," *Guardian*, December 7, 2012, Books section. http://www.theguardian.com/books/2012/dec/07/tombstone-mao-great-famine-yeng-jisheng-review, accessed October 30, 2015.

3   Edward Gibbon, *History of the Decline and Fall of the Roman Empire* (London: Strahan & Cadell, 1776–89).

4   Hannah Arendt, *Eichmann in Jerusalem: A Report on the Banality of Evil* (New York: Viking Press, 1963).

MODULE 8
PLACE IN THE AUTHOR'S WORK

KEY POINTS

- Frank Dikötter moved from researching social problems to writing positive histories of Republican China* (China in the period between 1912 and the coming to power of the Chinese Communist Party* [CCP] in 1949) to producing highly critical exposés of the whole Mao era (the period in which China was led by Mao Zedong).*

- *Mao's Great Famine* is the first book in an ambitious trilogy describing the ways in which the Mao era affected the lives of ordinary people over almost three decades.

- Based on four years of painstaking research, it is likely to be considered Dikötter's greatest achievement.

Positioning

Frank Dikötter's research falls into three eras, with *Mao's Great Famine: The History of China's Most Devastating Catastrophe* marking the beginning of the third. His first six books discussed marginalized groups and social problems in the following order: race; sex; medicine and eugenics (the science of "improving" human populations through sterilization and controlled breeding); birth defects; crime and prison; and drugs. He then took a more positive view with *Things Modern: Material Culture and Everyday Life in China* (2006).[1] This examines material culture in pre–communist* China, showing how the country was on a path to embracing modern global consumer culture.

In a logical next step, Dikötter explores China's republican era in *The Age of Openness: China Before Mao* (2008). He shows that Republican China, "far from being in a state of decay that called for revolutionary

> **❝** I have always been interested in how the best laid plans can go awry, for instance in the war on drugs. Is there a more devastating example of a utopian plan gone horribly wrong than the Great Leap Forward in 1958? **❞**
>
> Frank Dikötter, in Evan Osnos, "Q & A: Frank Dikötter on Famine and Mao," *New Yorker*

action, was in fact a vibrant and cosmopolitan society. In such a reading, the current Chinese leaders should not be seen as striving to do something bold and new; they are merely struggling to rebuild a network of global connections that Mao and others had systematically helped to destroy."[2] This quote on the dust jacket of Dikötter's book from the British American historian Jonathan Spence,* perhaps the most famous living historian of China, helps connect Dikötter's work on the Republican and Mao eras. On the surface, *Mao's Great Famine* may be seen as a departure from Dikötter's earlier works. Or maybe he is trying to explain what went wrong after the positive trends he identified in *Everyday Life in China* and *The Age of Openness*.

Integration

Mao's Great Famine sets Dikötter on a new and ambitious research path. It is intended to be the first of the *People's Trilogy*, a set of books assessing the impact of Mao-era communism on ordinary citizens of China. In 2013 he published the second part of the trilogy, *The Tragedy of Liberation: A History of the Chinese Revolution 1945–1957*.

The Tragedy of Liberation is perhaps best thought of as a prequel. It continues with many of the themes from *Mao's Great Famine*, but is set in the time before it. The book shows that "the first decade of Maoism was one of the worst tyrannies in the history of the twentieth century, sending to an early grave at least 5 million civilians and bringing misery to countless more." As the early Maoist period was often characterized as benevolent and productive, this was a fairly radical departure. In the words of the eminent China historian Rana Mitter,*[3] "this version of the PRC [People's Republic of China] is not a paradise lost: it was always hell."[4]

Dikötter's earlier books share some themes with the *People's Trilogy*. A concern with the use and abuse of state power runs through his work. *Sex, Culture and Modernity in China* (1995), for example, looks at how sex and sexuality increasingly became an object of investigation, surveillance, and intervention.[5] The trilogy does, however, mark a significant change of direction, but the explanation for this is practical: Dikötter grabbed the chance to analyze documents usually under lock and key. He explains that "most of all I wrote about Mao's Great Famine because in the years before the Beijing 2008 Olympics the party archives were quietly opening up, offering a real bounty of hitherto unseen party records: I saw an opportunity and I seized it."[6]

Significance

It is often the case that a scholar's first book is his or her best researched; first books are frequently the product of doctoral research, which tends to be extensive compared with research for later books. This is not true, however, for Dikötter, who, over the past 25 years, has slowly built a reputation as a leading historian. The *People's Trilogy* is certainly Dikötter's most ambitious project to date.

Mao's Great Famine is Dikötter's ninth book and likely to be seen as his greatest work. In comparison with the second book in the trilogy, *The Tragedy of Liberation*, *Mao's Great Famine* benefits from covering a more spectacular and better-known historical event. In it, Dikötter lays 45 million deaths at the feet of Mao and the CCP. *The Tragedy of Liberation*, by contrast, blames them for a "mere" 5 million deaths.[7]

The final book in the trilogy will be on the Cultural Revolution* (Mao's attempt to reassert his authority over the government). Once complete, it is possible the trilogy as a whole will eclipse *Mao's Great Famine* and the book will be seen as part of an excellent series providing a groundbreaking history of the entire Mao era.

NOTES

1 Frank Dikötter, *Things Modern: Material Culture and Everyday Life in China*. (London: C. Hurst & Co, 2006).

2 Frank Dikötter, *The Age of Openness: China before Mao* (Berkeley: University of California Press, 2008), dust jacket.

3 In the interest of full disclosure it should be noted that the author of this analysis studied under Professor Mitter at Oxford.

4 Rana Mitter, "*Tombstone: The Untold Story of Mao's Great Famine* by Yang Jisheng – Review," *Guardian*, December 7, 2012, Books section. http://www.theguardian.com/books/2012/dec/07/tombstone-mao-great-famine-yeng-jisheng-review, accessed October 30, 2015.

5 Frank Dikötter, *Sex, Culture, and Modernity in China: Medical Science and the Construction of Sexual Identities in the Early Republican Period* (Honolulu: University of Hawaii Press, 1995).

6 Evan Osnos, "Q & A: Frank Dikötter on Famine and Mao," *The New Yorker*, December 15, 2010. http://www.newyorker.com/news/evan-osnos/q-a-frank-diktter-on-famine-and-mao, accessed October 28, 2015.

7 Frank Dikötter, *The Tragedy of Liberation: A History of the Chinese Revolution 1945–1957* (New York: Bloomsbury Press, 2013), XIII.

SECTION 3
IMPACT

MODULE 9
THE FIRST RESPONSES

KEY POINTS

- *Mao's Great Famine* was criticized for listing grim anecdotes and examples without putting them into a historical or social context.

- Some critics argue that the text covers much of the same ground as the Chinese journalist Yang Jisheng's* 2008 book *Tombstone*.

- While both books paint the Great Chinese Famine* in bleak terms, *Mao's Great Famine* has outshone *Tombstone* as a more readable, conventional, and groundbreaking scholarly history.

Criticism

Some scholars viewed Frank Dikötter's *Mao's Great Famine: The History of China's Most Devastating Catastrophe* as retreading ground covered two years earlier by the journalist Yang Jisheng in *Tombstone* (2008). But *Tombstone* was originally published in Chinese, and not in English until 2012, so *Mao's Great Famine* was the first to present this story to the English-speaking world,[1] and in a more conventional history format.[2] The American journalist Ian Johnson* quipped that *Mao's Great Famine's* "primary contribution is to have been written in English, and in a conventional, linear narrative."[3]

The Irish economist Cormac Ó Gráda leveled fairly serious criticisms at *Mao's Great Famine* for being "more like a catalogue of anecdotes about atrocities than a sustained analytic argument."[4] He says Dikötter does not use the research to build a coherent argument about what happened and why; the book is, he claims, "dismissive of

> **‹‹** *Mao's Great Famine* has become the best-known
> account of the Great Leap Famine in our times. But
> should it be? **››**
>
> Cormac Ó Gráda,* *Eating People Is Wrong, and Other Essays on Famine,*
> *Its Past, and Its Future*

academic work on the topics … weak on context and unreliable with
data; and it fails to note that many of the horrors it describes were not
unique to 1959–61."[5] Ó Gráda accuses Dikötter of not providing
enough historical context to act as a fair point of comparison. For
example, many parents were forced to sell their children in exchange
for food. This practice had long been an accepted part of life for
China's poorest people, but Dikötter implies it was a new low.

Anthony Garnaut,* an Australia-based scholar of Islam in China,
argues that Dikötter uses "archival anecdotes stripped of geographic,
temporal, and institutional context."[6] This means it is difficult to
understand the incidents in the book in terms of the time and place
they happened. Garnaut claims that Dikötter "provides his readers
with a stream of vivid descriptions of suffering citizens neglected by
their leaders, interspersed with numerical lists of terrible things, which
are likely to generate discomfort on the part of the reader but not
comprehension."[7] He also implies that Dikötter owes an
unacknowledged debt to Yang Jisheng for copying his use of sources.

Responses

Towards the end of *Mao's Great Famine*, Dikötter makes sure he gets in
first with his take on any comparisons with *Tombstone*. Dikötter read
the book in Chinese and realized that once it was translated into
English, it would be a serious rival for the position of definitive history
of the famine. Dikötter attacks *Tombstone* by saying that "the book is
more of a compilation of notes from different sources than a carefully

constructed text. At times it looks like a hotchpotch which simply strings together large chunks of text, some lifted from the Web, a few from published sources, and others transcribed from archival material."[8] Dikötter continues in this dismissive tone, "Invaluable documents are thrown together with irrelevant anecdotes, making it difficult for the reader to see the wood for the trees. In some cases the author spent only a day or two in the archives, missing the most vital, and openly available, documents."[9] This seems to be a somewhat biased attack on the work of a fellow writer well regarded in his own right.[10] Dikötter's response to the accusation that he relies too heavily on Yang's sources is more reasonable—he compares specific sources and archives used by each of them to show that only a small subset of his sources overlapped with Yang's.[11]

Conflict And Consensus

Arguments over these books are mainly to do with differences in style and scholarly quibbling over the originality of sources. *Mao's Great Famine, Tombstone*, and Jasper Becker's* *Hungry Ghosts* may be very different in style and approach, but the picture they paint of the Great Leap Forward* and the Great Chinese Famine is essentially the same.

These texts forced a rethink of the era, but it is still difficult to dispel established views of the famine. The debate over just how many people died through starvation or murder has not been settled, with historians and officials offering different body counts. Dikötter's figure of a minimum of 45 million deaths has entered the conversation and is now included in almost every serious assessment of the Great Leap Forward and the Great Chinese Famine. Yet this figure tends to be included only alongside other lower numbers such as the official Chinese Communist Party's* figure of 15 million and Yang Jisheng's conservative estimate of 36 million. In the words of Ian Johnson, "Dikötter's number of deaths is a guesstimate, but a good one."[12]

In short, *Mao's Great Famine* has become the best-known account of the Great Leap Forward and the Great Chinese Famine and Dikötter's assessment of the era will continue to be important, if not totally dominant.

NOTES

1   Rana Mitter, "*Tombstone: The Untold Story of Mao's Great Famine* by Yang Jisheng – Review," *Guardian*, December 7, 2012, Books section. http://www.theguardian.com/books/2012/dec/07/tombstone-mao-great-famine-yeng-jisheng-review, accessed October 30, 2016.

2   Ian Johnson, "China: Worse Than You Ever Imagined," *The New York Review of Books*, November 22, 2012. http://www.nybooks.com/articles/archives/2012/nov/22/china-worse-you-ever-imagined/, accessed October 29, 2015.

3   Johnson, "China."

4   Cormac Ó Gráda, *Eating People Is Wrong, and Other Essays on Famine, Its Past, and Its Future* (Princeton, NJ: Princeton University Press, 2015), 134.

5   Ó Gráda, *Eating People Is Wrong,* 134.

6   Anthony Garnaut, "Hard Facts and Half-Truths: The New Archival History of China's Great Famine," *China Information* 27, no. 2 (July 1, 2013): 232, doi:10.1177/0920203X13485390.

7   Garnaut, "Hard Facts and Half-Truths," 232. Frank Dikötter, "Response to 'Hard Facts and Half-Truths: The New Archival History of China's Great Famine'." *China Information* 27, no. 3 (November 1, 2013): 371–8. doi:10.1177/0920203X13499856.

8   Frank Dikötter, *Mao's Great Famine: The History of China's Most Devastating Catastrophe, 1958–62* (London: Bloomsbury, 2010), 347.

9   Dikötter, *Mao's Great Famine,* 347.

10 Mitter, "*Tombstone.*"

11 Garnaut, "Hard Facts and Half-Truths."

12 Johnson, "China."

MODULE 10
THE EVOLVING DEBATE

KEY POINTS

- The impact of *Mao's Great Famine* is limited because the Great Leap Forward* and the Great Chinese Famine* are seen as tragedies for China rather than for all humanity.

- Thinking and writing on the era of Mao Zedong* spark passions across the political spectrum—from devoted communists* to people who want a smaller government.

- The book is not only a definitive account of the era for historians and China experts, it yields information for social scientists and even biologists.

Uses And Problems

Frank Dikötter's book *Mao's Great Famine: The History of China's Most Devastating Catastrophe* is the standard reference for anyone discussing the Great Leap Forward or the Great Chinese Famine. When a famous Chinese author recently published a novel set during the famine, for example, the media coverage included interviews with Dikötter.[1]

Despite this, the influence of *Mao's Great Famine* does not extend very far beyond the study of China. Most scholarly works that cite Dikötter focus exclusively on China or the issue of famine. Unlike the Holocaust* during World War II*—mourned as a universal tragedy— the famine tends to be seen as a specifically Chinese disaster. There are several reasons for this. They include Eurocentrism,* the fact that the tragedy was confined to one country, and the fact that the full horror of what happened was not known until decades later. If *Mao's Great Famine* could make the world understand the Great Chinese Famine as a universal human tragedy it would be a momentous

> **"**Tell me, how many books have you read about the Holocaust?"
>
> "Quite a few."
>
> "Quite a few."
>
> "How many books have you read about the Cultural Revolution?"*
>
> "Quite a few."
>
> "How many books have you read about the Great Leap Forward?"
>
> "Tens of millions of people died! There's one book by one journalist called Jasper Becker that was published 10 years ago. It's a subject crying out for more study. **"**
>
> Frank Dikötter and Matt Schiavenza, in Matt Schiavenza, "Interview: Frank Dikötter, Author of Mao's Great Famine," *asiasociety.org*

accomplishment. For now, it remains a central and much consulted work for those interested in China or famine.

Mao's Great Famine fuels the debate over the relationship between state and society under Mao. This questions how much effective control the Chinese government had over day-to-day life in the countryside. On one side of the debate is the American political scientist Vivienne Shue.*[2] In 1988, she published *The Reach of the State: Sketches of the Chinese Body Politic.* Her argument, highly controversial at the time, was that Mao's government did not actually achieve very high levels of control over rural Chinese society. She also argued that government policies often strengthened resistance against the state.[3]

On the other side of the argument are China experts such as the Australia-based journalist and scholar Jonathan Unger.* He says the

"Maoist state's grip on village affairs—politically, economically, and normatively—was, in fact, excruciatingly tight."[4]

Schools Of Thought

Mao's Great Famine is a modern history of a particular event and not the kind of book that can or even should lead to a broad school of thought. That said, it is a devastating exposé of communism—especially the Maoist* version. The actual practice of communism is fading across the world, even in countries such as China and Vietnam that still claim to be communist. *Mao's Great Famine* helps to explain why China's leaders continue to look to their Maoist past for legitimacy even as they allow their economy to be dominated by the market.

Staunch supporters of Mao and Maoism are likely to be violently opposed to *Mao's Great Famine*, just as Dikötter intended. Whatever intellectual argument can be made for communism, his book makes it virtually impossible to deny the disastrous consequences of central planning in the Great Leap Forward.

It is difficult for anyone involved in serious historical debate to defend Mao and Maoism, or communism as it existed in the Soviet Bloc* (the group of communist nations led by Russia) and China. The ideological gulf between people who have communist sympathies and those who do not still has the power to affect discussions about Mao and the China he created.

In Current Scholarship

Mao's Great Famine was published far too recently for Dikötter to be said yet to have influenced a generation of disciples or successors. Moreover, his research method (detailed and extensive research in local archives across China) may not be possible in the current political climate. In regard to this, journalist Tom Phillips has said: "In fact, access to government archives had become increasingly strict since Xi Jinping* came to power in late 2012, making it even harder for scholars researching the period."[5]

One slightly surprising place where the work is cited is in scientific research that focuses on issues related to famine. As a readable and reasonably comprehensive history of the famine, the book serves as an important resource for researchers. These studies have helped verify, for example, that women are more likely to give birth to girls than boys when they are exposed to extreme hunger.[6] *Mao's Great Famine* has been cited in books on everything from food culture[7] to the politics of authoritarian (dictatorial and undemocratic) rule.[8] Dikötter's graphic account is the standard reference for any scholar wresting with the Great Leap Forward and the famine it caused. The book provides an overwhelming sense of the catastrophic consequences of the over-zealous actions of the Chinese Communist Party* at the end of the 1950s and into the 1960s.

NOTES

1   Tom Phillips, "Author Throws Spotlight on China's 'Hidden Holocaust,'" *Telegraph*, March 25, 2015, World section. http://www.telegraph.co.uk/news/worldnews/asia/china/11495748/Author-throws-spotlight-on-Chinas-hidden-Holocaust.html, accessed December 1, 2015.

2   In the interest of full disclosure it should be noted that the author of this analysis studied under Professor Shue at Oxford.

3   Vivienne Shue, *The Reach of the State: Sketches of the Chinese Body Politic* (Stanford: Stanford University Press, 1988).

4   Jonathan Unger, "State and Peasant in Post Revolution China," *Journal of Peasant Studies* 17, no. 1 (1989): 114, doi:10.1080/03066158908438414.

5   Phillips, "Author Throws Spotlight on China's 'Hidden Holocaust.'"

6   Shige Song, "Does Famine Influence Sex Ratio at Birth? Evidence from the 1959–1961 Great Leap Forward Famine in China," *Proceedings of the Royal Society of London B: Biological Sciences*, March 28, 2012, rspb20120320, doi:10.1098/rspb.2012.0320.

7   E. N. Anderson, *Everyone Eats: Understanding Food and Culture,* Second Edition (New York: New York University Press, 2014).

8   Milan W. Svolik, *The Politics of Authoritarian Rule* (Cambridge University Press, 2012).

MODULE 11
IMPACT AND INFLUENCE TODAY

KEY POINTS

- *Mao's Great Famine* is the most famous and shocking account of the Great Leap Forward* and the Great Chinese Famine.*
- An honest and open reassessment of the era of the leadership of Mao Zedong* is difficult while China's repressive political climate remains.
- Further research into what really happened in China between 1958 and 1962 will have to wait until scholars are allowed to see all the records.

Position

That *Mao's Great Famine: The History of China's Most Devastating Catastrophe* beat stiff competition to emerge as the seminal and best-known history of the Great Leap Forward and the Great Chinese Famine is down to the scholarly credentials of its author Frank Dikötter, the meticulous research at its core, and its fairly readable tone. *Mao's Great Famine* is often used as an important source of knowledge about China, and not just among historians.

Fortune Magazine's China correspondent recommends *Mao's Great Famine* as one of "ten must-read books that explain modern China."[1] It is the only history book on the list. It is the authoritative text about its subject not only for history scholars, but also for social scientists (especially political scientists) and even researchers in the hard sciences (such as biology).

Another work may come along to take this position, but in China's current closed political climate it seems unlikely that another historian will gain the same access to the archives achieved by Dikötter. He or

> ❝ 'They [the Chinese Communist Party]* are in a
> pickle because once you start touching on Mao's Great
> Famine you can't just blame it on the Chairman,' he
> said. 'You will find out that just about every big shot
> had a hand in it.' ❞
>
> Frank Dikötter, in Tom Phillips, "Author Throws Spotlight on China's 'Hidden
> Holocaust'," *Telegraph*

she would need substantially greater access to the records to write a
book matching or surpassing *Mao's Great Famine* as the definitive
history of this turbulent era.

Mao's Great Famine remains a devastating and definitive take
on one of the twentieth century's most important but least
discussed subjects.

Interaction

Defenders of the Chinese Communist Party (CCP) and Chairman
Mao, especially those with a vested interest in protecting his legacy,
rarely if ever take part in serious intellectual discussion about the years
covered in *Mao's Great Famine*. Although people may argue about how
many tens of millions died, no serious historian claims the Great
Chinese Famine was anything other than an enormous and largely
man-made catastrophe. Indeed, "even the Communist Party was
forced to recognize that the famine was 70 percent man-made,"[2] and
even its official death toll of 15 million is staggering.

The sheer horror of the subject matter makes it easy to dismiss the
book's critics as apologists for Mao, even when their objections are
relatively mild. This can be in seen in a row between Dikötter and the
Indian writer Pankaj Mishra.* In a review for the *New Yorker*, Mishra
writes that "Dikötter is, indeed, generally dismissive of facts that could
blunt his story's sharp edge."[3] Dikötter's rather extreme response is

worth quoting at some length.

"I think Pankaj Mishra is clearly one of those old lefties who haven't quite gotten over the fact that socialism isn't the utopian paradise that it was promised to be. He's nostalgic for socialism. He's one of those who, despite whatever evidence you come up with, of the horrors and realities on the ground, will still find an excuse to tell you that Mao's rule wasn't that bad. He's like one of these people who goes around telling you that Adolf Hitler built highways or solved the inflation problem. It's called denial. Denial and apologia."[4]

In response Mishra writes:"I am not sure why these mild objections to his book should provoke such an intemperate outburst from Dikötter."[5] The answer seems to be that communism* still has the ability to raise even scholarly tempers.

The Continuing Debate

Mao's Great Famine has an important place in a larger project shared by many scholars to force the CCP to face up to its past. The American commentator Ian Johnson* sums up this movement when discussing Yang Jisheng's *Tombstone*, a study that covers the same events as *Mao's Great Famine*: "It would be simplistic to say *Tombstone* alone has set off this rethinking of Chinese history. Instead, like any great book it is part of something bigger, in this case a desire by many Chinese people to reconsider their society's future by clarifying its past."[6]

As a more popular and readable volume, *Mao's Great Famine* has an even more important role to play in the reevaluation of China's past and future. Yet within China, where making sense of the past needs to happen, these vital works are largely banned. Dikötter recognizes this difficult reality, saying in an interview with Tom Phillips, "President Xi has made it pretty clear that there should be no attempt to discredit the Communist Party and its history."[7] An honest evaluation of China's history may not come until people are allowed to openly discuss the past inside the country itself. Until then, *Mao's Great Famine* will remain largely unknown to its most important audience—the Chinese people.

NOTES

1   Scott Cendrowski, "Ten Must-Read Books that Explain Modern China," *Fortune Magazine*, April 4, 2015. http://fortune.com/2015/04/04/china-modern-economy-10-books/, accessed January 13, 2016.

2   Bloomberg News, "Cannibal China, Starved by Mao, Ate Earth, Robbed Graves: Books," *Bloomberg.com*. http://www.bloomberg.com/news/articles/2010-08–29/cannibal-chinese-starved-by-mao-ate-earth-bartered-sex-for-food-books, accessed October 29, 2015.

3   Pankaj Mishra, "Staying Power," *The New Yorker*, December 20, 2010, http://www.newyorker.com/magazine/2010/12/20/staying-power-3.

4   Matt Schiavenza, "Interview: Frank Dikötter, Author of Mao's Great Famine[UPDATED]," *Asia Society*. http://asiasociety.org/blog/asia/interview-frank-dik%C3%B6tter-author-maos-great-famine-updated, accessed October 30, 2015.

5   Schiavenza, "Interview."

6   Ian Johnson, "China: Worse Than You Ever Imagined," *The New York Review of Books*, November 22, 2012. http://www.nybooks.com/articles/archives/2012/nov/22/china-worse-you-ever-imagined/, accessed October 29, 2015.

7   Tom Phillips, "Author Throws Spotlight on China's 'Hidden Holocaust,'" *Telegraph*, March 25, 2015, World section. http://www.telegraph.co.uk/news/worldnews/asia/china/11495748/Author-throws-spotlight-on-Chinas-hidden-Holocaust.html, accessed December 1, 2015.

MODULE 12
WHERE NEXT?

KEY POINTS

- The task of evaluating the Maoist* era is complicated by "princelings"—the descendants of Chinese Communist Party* (CCP) officials from Mao Zedong's* day who hold powerful positions in modern China.

- The Chinese translation of *Mao's Great Famine* was only published in Taiwan and Hong Kong and the clampdown on further research into the archives continues, making it difficult for scholars to reveal more about the Great Leap Forward.*

- Frank Dikötter has written the best-known account of possibly the greatest man-made tragedy in history and calls for a complete and honest account of what happened—something that is unlikely to happen under the enduring communist* regime.

Potential

Mao's Great Famine: The History of China's Most Devastating Catastrophe by Frank Dikötter plays a crucial role in advancing our understanding of the mass starvation caused by the Great Leap Forward, China's disastrous attempt to industrialize at speed from the late 1950s. The big obstacle to delving further into these events, however, is China's closed political environment. The CCP is firmly entrenched, and with no signs of the country's leaders moving toward any kind of political opening up, this situation is unlikely to change soon.

The increasing importance of "princelings" in China makes the famine and the state policies that spawned it even more contentious. "Princelings" are the descendants of high-level communist officials of

> 66 Future historians, hopefully, will be able to reveal
> the true scale of what happened on the basis of fully
> open archives. 99
>
> Frank Dikötter, *Mao's Great Famine: The History of China's Most Devastating Catastrophe*

Mao's generation—politicians in powerful positions related to the people who might have had a hand in the disaster of the Great Chinese Famine.*[1] Many of these forebears are actually named and shamed in *Mao's Great Famine*.

Reports that cast a negative light on Chinese leaders (along with the newspapers that publish them) prompt swift negative responses by the state.[2] It would be easier for the CCP to accept a critical reappraisal of leaders of the Mao era if their descendants were not in such positions of prominence throughout Chinese society.

Future Directions

Mao's Great Famine, along with the Chinese journalist Yang Jisheng's* *Tombstone* and a few other studies, has achieved most of what is possible under the clampdown on access to CCP archives. Work that improves on these texts is unlikely to emerge until a historian is allowed proper access to these sources, and this does not seem likely to happen any time soon. Dikötter managed to get his research done during a rare window of openness in the lead-up to the Beijing Olympics in 2008. The period since the games has been primarily one of closing up again.

Yet nothing can stay hidden away forever. Even another small political opening, like the one Dikötter enjoyed, could be enough for a new generation of historians to mine the material that tells the story of the Great Leap Forward and the Great Chinese Famine. Dikötter's statistic of 45 million deaths is a loose estimate[3] not based on rigorous sampling and statistical techniques.[4] In the hands of future scholars, more sophisticated methods could provide a much more precise idea of the scale of death and damage.

Mao's Great Famine was translated into Chinese in 2011, but the translation was only published in Taiwan and Hong Kong. Its lack of availability makes it fairly easy to ignore in China. Someday a more honest reconsideration of the Mao era will occur in mainland China. When that day comes, *Mao's Great Famine* is likely to be at the heart of the debate. It may be attacked by supporters of Mao and the Chinese Communist Party, but it seems likely to stand the test of time as an important history of this extraordinary period.

Summary

Mao's Great Famine is the most famous and readable account of possibly the greatest man-made tragedy in world history—a catastrophe that most know little or nothing about. Based on extensive and painstaking research through generally closed archives, it documents the horrors of the Great Leap Forward and the Great Chinese Famine. The book carefully and relentlessly illustrates the terrible consequences for ordinary people. The disaster drove whole swathes of the population to starvation and acts of unimaginable desperation such as cannibalism and selling children in exchange for food. Frank Dikötter puts the death toll at 45 million, three times the official number.

While Dikötter places much of the blame for all this at the feet of Mao Zedong, there is plenty more to go around. He shows that all the way down the line, from top Chinese leaders to the person dishing out gruel in the village, a huge number of people had to do a great number of awful things (often out of desperation) for the famine to become the catastrophe that it was.

Mao's Great Famine has become the most significant history of these events. It calls for nothing less than a serious reevaluation of the entire Mao era—but in China's closed political environment it seems unlikely that such a radical review of history is possible.

NOTES

1   Cheng Li, "China's New Leaders: Rule of the Princelings," *The Brookings Institution*. http://www.brookings.edu/research/articles/2013/02/china-xi-jinping-li, accessed October 29, 2015.

2   "Chinese Premier's Family Has Massive Wealth: NYT Report," *Reuters*, October 26, 2012. http://www.reuters.com/article/2012/10/26/us-china-wen-wealth-idUSBRE89P05320121026, accessed October 30, 2015.

3   Ian Johnson, "China: Worse Than You Ever Imagined," *The New York Review of Books*, November 22, 2012. http://www.nybooks.com/articles/archives/2012/nov/22/china-worse-you-ever-imagined/, accessed October 29, 2015.

4   Anthony Garnaut, "Hard Facts and Half-Truths: The New Archival History of China's Great Famine," China Information 27, no. 2 (July 1, 2013): 232, doi:10.1177/0920203X13485390.

GLOSSARY

GLOSSARY OF TERMS

Armenian Genocide: the systematic extermination in 1915 of ethnic Armenians in what is today Turkey, conducted by agents of the ruling Ottoman dynasty. The total death toll was estimated at between 800,000 and 1.5 million.

Auschwitz: a network of concentration camps built and operated by Nazi Germany in areas of Poland annexed during World War II.

Cambodian Genocide: a genocide carried out by the communist Khmer Rouge political party between 1975 and 1979. The regime led by its leader Pol Pot killed an estimated one and a half to three million people.

Cannibalism: the practice or act of a human eating the body parts of other humans.

Chinese Civil War: a war fought between the Nationalist Kuomintang government and the Communist Party of China. The most important phase lasted from the end of Japanese occupation in 1945 until the communist victory in 1949.

Chinese Communist Party (CCP): a militarized communist party that gained control over China after the Chinese Civil War in 1949. It has ruled China ever since.

Cold War: a heightened state of political, diplomatic, and military tension between the United States and its allies and the Soviet Union and its allies; it lasted approximately from the end of World War II in 1945 until the fall of the Soviet Union in 1991.

Collectivization: an important part of communist agricultural policy. In this process, farmers were made to combine their individual farms into larger collective farms that were generally owned and managed by the state.

Communism: a political and economic ideology and movement that espouses the superiority of a society based on the common ownership of the means of production.

Cultural Revolution: a Chinese social–political movement that ran from 1966 until 1976 (when Mao Zedong died). Orchestrated by Mao, it threw the Chinese Communist Party and the country into chaos.

Eurocentrism: a worldview centered on Western civilization that tends to overlook important events and contributions from other parts of the world.

Genocide: the systematic elimination of a specific group of people, generally chosen on grounds of race, ethnicity, religion, culture, nationality, or political affiliation.

Great Chinese Famine: the greatest famine in human history. Caused in large part by government policies, it lasted from 1958 to 1961 and resulted in tens of millions of deaths.

Great Leap Forward: a campaign by the Chinese Communist Party that ran from 1958 to 1961, and was intended to jumpstart China's industrialization and overtake Britain in production of steel and other products within 15 years.

Holocaust: the worst genocide in history. Adolf Hitler's Nazi regime and its collaborators killed approximately six million Jews and five million non-Jews, especially ethnic Poles, homosexuals, Romani, and the disabled.

Iron Curtain: the name given to the boundary between communist and noncommunist countries during the Cold War, especially in Europe.

Khmer Rouge: the ruling party in Cambodia from 1975 to 1979. Led by Pol Pot, the party is best remembered as the perpetrator of the Cambodian Genocide.

Kuomintang (KMT): the Chinese Nationalist Party that governed most of China from 1928 to 1949, when it lost the Chinese Civil War to the Communists. The KMT then escaped to Taiwan and has ruled that island for most of the period since 1949.

Maoism: the branch of communist ideology created by Mao Zedong that emphasizes guerrilla warfare and focuses on peasants rather than workers as a potential revolutionary class. It has become different since Mao died in 1976, but some groups of rural guerrilla fighters, primarily in Asia and Latin America, have adopted the ideology.

Nazi Party: an extreme right-wing political party in Germany that was active between 1920 and 1945. It was in power during World War II and perpetrated the Holocaust.

Ottoman Empire: based in modern Turkey from 1299 to 1923. At its height it extended over much of southeast Europe, western Asia, the Caucasus, and North Africa.

Republican China: a number of governments that ruled China between the fall of the Qing Dynasty in 1912 and the Communists' 1949 victory in the Chinese Civil War.

Revisionist history: history that reinterprets the historical record. It reviews events and motives, changing orthodox views of history.

Social history: a broad category of historical research that emerged especially in the 1960s and 1970s. It focuses on the experiences and circumstances of ordinary people.

Soviet Bloc: the group of communist nations closely allied with the Soviet Union during the Cold War. These generally include Bulgaria, Cuba, Czechoslovakia, East Germany, Hungary, Poland, and Romania.

Soviet famine of 1932–3: a famine that affected most of the Soviet Union's major grain-producing regions. It led to millions of deaths and was linked to the forced collectivization of agriculture.

Soviet Union: a federation of countries in Eastern Europe and Asia, founded on communist principles, which collapsed in 1991.

Stalin's purges (1936–8): also known as the Great Purge or the Great Terror. This was a Soviet campaign of political repression including imprisonment, labor camps, and arbitrary executions that targeted Communist Party and government officials, peasants, and Soviet army officers.

Tiananmen Square massacre: In 1989, student-led demonstrations broke out in Beijing. After almost seven weeks the Chinese government sent in the military to repress the protest, killing hundreds or perhaps even thousands of civilians.

Weapons of the weak: a concept created by the political scientist and anthropologist James Scott, which recognizes the ways that even the least powerful individuals resist domination. Examples include stealing small amounts of food and deserting from military service.

World War II: a war fought primarily from 1939 to 1945, though it included other earlier conflicts, such as the Japanese invasion of China. It involved over 100 million combatants and more than 30 countries. It was the most widespread and deadly conflict in history.

PEOPLE MENTIONED IN THE TEXT

Hannah Arendt (1906–75) was a German-born political theorist and philosopher who escaped Europe during the Holocaust. She is best known for her books *The Origins of Totalitarianism* and *Eichmann in Jerusalem*.

Jasper Becker (b. 1956) is a British journalist who specializes in China. He is perhaps best known for his book about the Great Leap Forward, *Hungry Ghosts*.

Jung Chang (b. 1952) is a Chinese-born British writer. She is best known for her family autobiography *Wild Swans*.

Chen Yizi (1940–2014) was a Chinese Communist Party official who helped reshape China's economy in 1980. He fled to the United States in the wake of his support for the Tiananmen Square protests.

Deng Xiaoping (1904–97) was a Chinese communist leader. After Mao's death he became the most powerful leader in the People's Republic of China. He reversed the course of Mao's policies and set China on its current path of economic liberalization.

Anthony Garnaut (b. 1977) is an Australian scholar of Chinese history. He has been a lecturer at the University of Melbourne, Australia, and a lecturer and research fellow in Chinese history at the University of Oxford.

Edward Gibbon (1737–94) was a member of Britain's Parliament and a notable historian. He is best known for his six-volume *History of the Decline and Fall of the Roman Empire*.

Jon Halliday is an Irish historian and modern Asia specialist. He is perhaps best known for his book *Mao: The Unknown Story*.

Eric Hobsbawm (1917–2012) was a Marxist historian. He is best known for his trilogy about the "long nineteenth century"—works considering the culture, politics, economy, and society of Europe in the final decades of the eighteenth century and the nineteenth century.

Ian Johnson (Zhang Yan) (b. 1962) is a writer and journalist, formerly for the *Wall Street Journal*. He is perhaps best known for his book about resistance to the Chinese State, *Wild Grass: Three Stories of Change in Modern China*.

Primo Levi (1919–87) was an Italian Jewish scientist and writer. He is perhaps best known for his 1947 book *If This Is a Man*, an account of the time he spent as a prisoner in one of the Auschwitz concentration camps.

Li Zhisui (1919–95) was Mao Zedong's personal physician and confidant. He is best known for publishing a biography entitled *The Private Life of Chairman Mao*.

Roderick MacFarquhar (b. 1930) is a historian and China expert, former member of Britain's Parliament, and journalist. He is best known for his three-part history of the Chinese Cultural Revolution, *The Origins of the Cultural Revolution*.

Mao Zedong (1893–1976) was a communist revolutionary in China. He helped found the People's Republic of China and was chairman of the Communist Party of China, and hence its supreme leader, from its foundation in 1949 until his death.

Pankaj Mishra (b. 1969) is an Indian novelist and nonfiction author. He is perhaps best known for his book *From the Ruins of Empire: The Intellectuals Who Remade Asia*, which won the Leipzig Book Prize for European Understanding.

Rana Mitter (b. 1969) is a British historian of Republican China, a radio presenter, and a professor of politics and history at the University of Oxford. He is best known for his book *A Bitter Revolution: China's Struggle with the Modern World*.

Cormac Ó Gráda (b. 1945) is an Irish famine scholar, and a professor of economics at University College Dublin. He is perhaps best known for his book *Black '47 and Beyond: The Great Irish Famine in History, Economy, and Memory*.

James Scott (b. 1936) is the Sterling Professor of Political Science at Yale University. He is best known for his book *Weapons of the Weak: Everyday Forms of Peasant Resistance*.

Gary Sheffield (b. 1961) is an English scholar of World War I and a frequent media commentator. He is perhaps best known for his book *The Chief: Douglas Haig and the British Army*.

Vivienne Shue (b. 1944) is a professor emeritus of contemporary China studies and associate of the University of Oxford China Centre. She is best known for her 1988 book *The Reach of the State: Sketches of the Chinese Body Politic*.

Jonathan Spence (b. 1936) is a professor of Chinese History. He is best known for his books *The Death of Woman Wang* (1978) and *The Question of Hu* (1987).

Joseph Stalin (1878–1953) was the leader of the Soviet Union from the mid-1920s until his death. He is considered responsible for the deaths of many millions of people as a consequence of agricultural policy and political repression.

Jonathan Unger (b. 1946) is a journalist and a professor at Australia National University. He is best known for his book *The Transformation of Rural China*.

Xi Jinping (b. 1953) is currently China's "paramount leader" as president of the People's Republic of China, general secretary of the Communist Party of China, and chairman of the Central Military Commission.

Yang Jisheng (b. 1940) is a Chinese journalist. He is best known for his book *Tombstone* about the Great Leap Forward and the Great Chinese Famine.

Howard Zinn (1922–2010) was an American playwright, social activist, and political scientist. He is best known for his revisionist history of the United States, *A People's History of the United States*.

WORKS CITED

WORKS CITED

Anderson, E. N. *Everyone Eats: Understanding Food and Culture, Second Edition*. New York: New York University Press, 2014.

Arendt, Hannah. *Eichmann in Jerusalem: A Report on the Banality of Evil*. New York: Viking Press, 1963.

Bachman, David. *Bureaucracy, Economy, and Leadership in China: The Institutional Origins of the Great Leap Forward*. Cambridge University Press, 2006.

Becker, Jasper. *Hungry Ghosts: Mao's Secret Famine*. New York: Macmillan, 1998.

Bianco, Lucien. "Frank Dikötter, Mao's Great Famine, The History of China's Most Devastating Catastrophe, 1958–62." Translated by N. Jayaram. *China Perspectives*, no. 2011/2 (July 30, 2011): 74–5.

Bloomberg News. "Cannibal China, Starved by Mao, Ate Earth, Robbed Graves: Books." *Bloomberg.com*. Accessed October 29, 2015. www.bloomberg.com/news/articles/2010-08-29/cannibal-chinese-starved-by-mao-ate-earth-bartered-sex-for-food-books.

Brzeski, Patrick. "Catching up with the Past." *South China Morning Post*, September 4, 2011. www.frankdikotter.com/interviews/patrick-brzeski.html. Accessed October 21, 2015.

Cendrowski, Scott. "Ten Must-Read Books that Explain Modern China." *Fortune Magazine*, April 4, 2015. Accessed January 13, 2016. http://fortune.com/2015/04/04/china-modern-economy-10-books/.

Chan, Alfred L. *Mao's Crusade: Politics and Policy Implementation in China's Great Leap Forward*. Oxford: Oxford University Press, 2001.

"Chinese Premier's Family Has Massive Wealth: NYT Report." *Reuters*, October 26, 2012. Accessed October 30, 2015. www.reuters.com/article/2012/10/26/us-china-wen-wealth-idUSBRE89P05320121026.

"Chinese Reopen Debate Over Mao's Legacy." *NPR.org*. www.npr.org/2011/06/22/137231508/chinese-reopen-debate-over-chairman-maos-legacy. Accessed October 23, 2015.

Dikötter, Frank. *The Age of Openness: China Before Mao*. Berkeley: University of California Press, 2008.

"Frank Dikötter's Professional Website." Accessed October 22, 2015, www.frankdikotter.com/.

Mao's Great Famine: The History of China's Most Devastating Catastrophe, 1958–62. London: Bloomsbury, 2010.

"Response to 'Hard Facts and Half-Truths: The New Archival History of China's Great Famine'." *China Information* 27, no. 3 (November 1, 2013): 371–8. doi:10.1177/0920203X13499856.

Sex, Culture, and Modernity in China: Medical Science and the Construction of Sexual Identities in the Early Republican Period. Honolulu: University of Hawaii Press, 1995.

Things Modern: Material Culture and Everyday Life in China. London: C. Hurst & Co, 2006.

The Tragedy of Liberation: A History of the Chinese Revolution 1945–1957. New York: Bloomsbury Press, 2013.

Fathers, Michael. "A Most Secret Tragedy." *Wall Street Journal*, October 26, 2012, Life and Style section. Accessed January 22, 2016. www.wsj.com/articles/SB10000872396390444180004578015170039623486.

Garnaut, Anthony. "Hard Facts and Half-Truths: The New Archival History of China's Great Famine." *China Information* 27, no. 2 (July 1, 2013): 223–46. doi:10.1177/0920203X13485390.

Gibbon, Edward. *History of the Decline and Fall of the Roman Empire.* London: Strahan & Cadell, 1776–89.

Johnson, Ian. "China: Worse Than You Ever Imagined." *The New York Review of Books*, November 22, 2012. Accessed October 29, 2015. www.nybooks.com/articles/archives/2012/nov/22/china-worse-you-ever-imagined/.

Kammen, Michael. "How the Other Half Lived." *Washington Post Book World*, 23 March 1980, 7.

Li, Cheng. "China's New Leaders: Rule of the Princelings." *The Brookings Institution*. Accessed October 29, 2015. www.brookings.edu/research/articles/2013/02/china-xi-jinping-li.

Lin, Justin Yifu, and Dennis Tao Yang. "On the Causes of China's Agricultural Crisis and the Great Leap Famine." *China Economic Review* 9, no. 2 (1998), China's Great Famine: 125–40. doi:10.1016/S1043-951X(99)80010-8.

Li Zhisui. *The Private Life of Chairman Mao.* New York: Random House, 2011.

MacFarquhar, Roderick. *The Origins of the Cultural Revolution, Volume 2.* London: Columbia University Press, 1983.

Mao Zedong. *The Little Red Book.*

McDonald, Forest. *Recovering the Past: A Historian's Memoir.* Lawrence: University Press of Kansas, 2004.

Mishra, Pankaj. "Staying Power." *The New Yorker*, December 20, 2010. www.newyorker.com/magazine/2010/12/20/staying-power-3.

Mitter, Rana. "*Tombstone: The Untold Story of Mao's Great Famine* by Yang Jisheng – Review." *Guardian*, December 7, 2012, Books section. Accessed October 30, 2015. www.theguardian.com/books/2012/dec/07/tombstone-mao-great-famine-yeng-jisheng-review.

Nathan, Andrew. "Jade and Plastic." *London Review of Books*, November 17, 2005.

Gráda, Cormac Ó. *Eating People Is Wrong, and Other Essays on Famine, Its Past, and Its Future*. Princeton, NJ: Princeton University Press, 2015.

Osnos, Evan. "Q. & A.: Frank Dikötter on Famine and Mao." *The New Yorker*, December 15, 2010. Accessed October 28, 2015. www.newyorker.com/news/evan-osnos/q-a-frank-diktter-on-famine-and-mao.

Phillips, Tom. "Author Throws Spotlight on China's 'Hidden Holocaust.'" *Telegraph*, March 25, 2015, World section. Accessed December 1, 2015. www.telegraph.co.uk/news/worldnews/asia/china/11495748/Author-throws-spotlight-on-Chinas-hidden-Holocaust.html.

Rosefielde, Steven. "Documented Homicides and Excess Deaths: New Insights into the Scale of Killing in the USSR during the 1930s." *Communist and Post-Communist Studies* 30, no. 3 (September 1997): 321–31. doi:10.1016/S0967-067X(97)00011-1.

Rummel, Rudolph J. "Power, Genocide and Mass Murder." *Journal of Peace Research* 31, no. 1 (February 1994): 1–10.

Schiavenza, Matt. "Interview: Frank Dikötter, Author of Mao's Great Famine [UPDATED]." *Asia Society*. Accessed October 30, 2015. http:/asiasociety.org/blog/asia/interview-frank-dik%C3%B6tter-author-maos-great-famine-updated.

Scott, James C. "Weapons of the Weak: Everyday Forms of Peasant Resistance." New Haven, CT: Yale University Press, 1985.

Sheffield, Gary. "The Western Front: Lions Led by Donkeys?" BBC.com. Accessed January 21, 2016, www.bbc.co.uk/history/worldwars/wwone/lions_donkeys_01.shtml

Shue, Vivienne. *The Reach of the State: Sketches of the Chinese Body Politic*. Stanford: Stanford University Press, 1988.

Song, Shige. "Does Famine Influence Sex Ratio at Birth? Evidence from the 1959–1961 Great Leap Forward Famine in China." *Proceedings of the Royal Society of London B: Biological Sciences*, March 28, 2012, rspb20120320. doi:10.1098/rspb.2012.0320.

Svolik, Milan W. *The Politics of Authoritarian Rule*. Cambridge: Cambridge University Press, 2012.

Unger, Jonathan. "State and Peasant in Post-RevolutionChina."*Journal of Peasant Studies* 17, no. 1 (1989): 114–36 doi:10.1080/03066158908438414.

Wood, James. "The Art of Witness." *The New Yorker*, September 28, 2015. www.newyorker.com/magazine/2015/09/28/the-art-of-witness. Accessed 27 October 2015.

Yang Jisheng. *Tombstone: The Untold Story of Mao's Great Famine*. London: Allen Lane, 2012 (originally published in Chinese in 2008).

THE MACAT LIBRARY
BY DISCIPLINE

AFRICANA STUDIES

Chinua Achebe's *An Image of Africa: Racism in Conrad's Heart of Darkness*
W. E. B. Du Bois's *The Souls of Black Folk*
Zora Neale Huston's *Characteristics of Negro Expression*
Martin Luther King Jr's *Why We Can't Wait*
Toni Morrison's *Playing in the Dark: Whiteness in the American Literary Imagination*

ANTHROPOLOGY

Arjun Appadurai's *Modernity at Large: Cultural Dimensions of Globalisation*
Philippe Ariès's *Centuries of Childhood*
Franz Boas's *Race, Language and Culture*
Kim Chan & Renée Mauborgne's *Blue Ocean Strategy*
Jared Diamond's *Guns, Germs & Steel: the Fate of Human Societies*
Jared Diamond's *Collapse: How Societies Choose to Fail or Survive*
E. E. Evans-Pritchard's *Witchcraft, Oracles and Magic Among the Azande*
James Ferguson's *The Anti-Politics Machine*
Clifford Geertz's *The Interpretation of Cultures*
David Graeber's *Debt: the First 5000 Years*
Karen Ho's *Liquidated: An Ethnography of Wall Street*
Geert Hofstede's *Culture's Consequences: Comparing Values, Behaviors, Institutes and Organizations across Nations*
Claude Lévi-Strauss's *Structural Anthropology*
Jay Macleod's *Ain't No Makin' It: Aspirations and Attainment in a Low-Income Neighborhood*
Saba Mahmood's *The Politics of Piety: The Islamic Revival and the Feminist Subject*
Marcel Mauss's *The Gift*

BUSINESS

Jean Lave & Etienne Wenger's *Situated Learning*
Theodore Levitt's *Marketing Myopia*
Burton G. Malkiel's *A Random Walk Down Wall Street*
Douglas McGregor's *The Human Side of Enterprise*
Michael Porter's *Competitive Strategy: Creating and Sustaining Superior Performance*
John Kotter's *Leading Change*
C. K. Prahalad & Gary Hamel's *The Core Competence of the Corporation*

CRIMINOLOGY

Michelle Alexander's *The New Jim Crow: Mass Incarceration in the Age of Colorblindness*
Michael R. Gottfredson & Travis Hirschi's *A General Theory of Crime*
Richard Herrnstein & Charles A. Murray's *The Bell Curve: Intelligence and Class Structure in American Life*
Elizabeth Loftus's *Eyewitness Testimony*
Jay Macleod's *Ain't No Makin' It: Aspirations and Attainment in a Low-Income Neighborhood*
Philip Zimbardo's *The Lucifer Effect*

ECONOMICS

Janet Abu-Lughod's *Before European Hegemony*
Ha-Joon Chang's *Kicking Away the Ladder*
David Brion Davis's *The Problem of Slavery in the Age of Revolution*
Milton Friedman's *The Role of Monetary Policy*
Milton Friedman's *Capitalism and Freedom*
David Graeber's *Debt: the First 5000 Years*
Friedrich Hayek's *The Road to Serfdom*
Karen Ho's *Liquidated: An Ethnography of Wall Street*

John Maynard Keynes's *The General Theory of Employment, Interest and Money*
Charles P. Kindleberger's *Manias, Panics and Crashes*
Robert Lucas's *Why Doesn't Capital Flow from Rich to Poor Countries?*
Burton G. Malkiel's *A Random Walk Down Wall Street*
Thomas Robert Malthus's *An Essay on the Principle of Population*
Karl Marx's *Capital*
Thomas Piketty's *Capital in the Twenty-First Century*
Amartya Sen's *Development as Freedom*
Adam Smith's *The Wealth of Nations*
Nassim Nicholas Taleb's *The Black Swan: The Impact of the Highly Improbable*
Amos Tversky's & Daniel Kahneman's *Judgment under Uncertainty: Heuristics and Biases*
Mahbub Ul Haq's *Reflections on Human Development*
Max Weber's *The Protestant Ethic and the Spirit of Capitalism*

FEMINISM AND GENDER STUDIES

Judith Butler's *Gender Trouble*
Simone De Beauvoir's *The Second Sex*
Michel Foucault's *History of Sexuality*
Betty Friedan's *The Feminine Mystique*
Saba Mahmood's *The Politics of Piety: The Islamic Revival and the Feminist Subject*
Joan Wallach Scott's *Gender and the Politics of History*
Mary Wollstonecraft's *A Vindication of the Rights of Woman*
Virginia Woolf's *A Room of One's Own*

GEOGRAPHY

The Brundtland Report's *Our Common Future*
Rachel Carson's *Silent Spring*
Charles Darwin's *On the Origin of Species*
James Ferguson's *The Anti-Politics Machine*
Jane Jacobs's *The Death and Life of Great American Cities*
James Lovelock's *Gaia: A New Look at Life on Earth*
Amartya Sen's *Development as Freedom*
Mathis Wackernagel & William Rees's *Our Ecological Footprint*

HISTORY

Janet Abu-Lughod's *Before European Hegemony*
Benedict Anderson's *Imagined Communities*
Bernard Bailyn's *The Ideological Origins of the American Revolution*
Hanna Batatu's *The Old Social Classes And The Revolutionary Movements Of Iraq*
Christopher Browning's *Ordinary Men: Reserve Police Batallion 101 and the Final Solution in Poland*
Edmund Burke's *Reflections on the Revolution in France*
William Cronon's *Nature's Metropolis: Chicago And The Great West*
Alfred W. Crosby's *The Columbian Exchange*
Hamid Dabashi's *Iran: A People Interrupted*
David Brion Davis's *The Problem of Slavery in the Age of Revolution*
Nathalie Zemon Davis's *The Return of Martin Guerre*
Jared Diamond's *Guns, Germs & Steel: the Fate of Human Societies*
Frank Dikotter's *Mao's Great Famine*
John W Dower's *War Without Mercy: Race And Power In The Pacific War*
W. E. B. Du Bois's *The Souls of Black Folk*
Richard J. Evans's *In Defence of History*
Lucien Febvre's *The Problem of Unbelief in the 16th Century*
Sheila Fitzpatrick's *Everyday Stalinism*

Eric Foner's *Reconstruction: America's Unfinished Revolution, 1863-1877*
Michel Foucault's *Discipline and Punish*
Michel Foucault's *History of Sexuality*
Francis Fukuyama's *The End of History and the Last Man*
John Lewis Gaddis's *We Now Know: Rethinking Cold War History*
Ernest Gellner's *Nations and Nationalism*
Eugene Genovese's *Roll, Jordan, Roll: The World the Slaves Made*
Carlo Ginzburg's *The Night Battles*
Daniel Goldhagen's *Hitler's Willing Executioners*
Jack Goldstone's *Revolution and Rebellion in the Early Modern World*
Antonio Gramsci's *The Prison Notebooks*
Alexander Hamilton, John Jay & James Madison's *The Federalist Papers*
Christopher Hill's *The World Turned Upside Down*
Carole Hillenbrand's *The Crusades: Islamic Perspectives*
Thomas Hobbes's *Leviathan*
Eric Hobsbawm's *The Age Of Revolution*
John A. Hobson's *Imperialism: A Study*
Albert Hourani's *History of the Arab Peoples*
Samuel P. Huntington's *The Clash of Civilizations and the Remaking of World Order*
C. L. R. James's *The Black Jacobins*
Tony Judt's *Postwar: A History of Europe Since 1945*
Ernst Kantorowicz's *The King's Two Bodies: A Study in Medieval Political Theology*
Paul Kennedy's *The Rise and Fall of the Great Powers*
Ian Kershaw's *The "Hitler Myth": Image and Reality in the Third Reich*
John Maynard Keynes's *The General Theory of Employment, Interest and Money*
Charles P. Kindleberger's *Manias, Panics and Crashes*
Martin Luther King Jr's *Why We Can't Wait*
Henry Kissinger's *World Order: Reflections on the Character of Nations and the Course of History*
Thomas Kuhn's *The Structure of Scientific Revolutions*
Georges Lefebvre's *The Coming of the French Revolution*
John Locke's *Two Treatises of Government*
Niccolò Machiavelli's *The Prince*
Thomas Robert Malthus's *An Essay on the Principle of Population*
Mahmood Mamdani's *Citizen and Subject: Contemporary Africa And The Legacy Of Late Colonialism*
Karl Marx's *Capital*
Stanley Milgram's *Obedience to Authority*
John Stuart Mill's *On Liberty*
Thomas Paine's *Common Sense*
Thomas Paine's *Rights of Man*
Geoffrey Parker's *Global Crisis: War, Climate Change and Catastrophe in the Seventeenth Century*
Jonathan Riley-Smith's *The First Crusade and the Idea of Crusading*
Jean-Jacques Rousseau's *The Social Contract*
Joan Wallach Scott's *Gender and the Politics of History*
Theda Skocpol's *States and Social Revolutions*
Adam Smith's *The Wealth of Nations*
Timothy Snyder's *Bloodlands: Europe Between Hitler and Stalin*
Sun Tzu's *The Art of War*
Keith Thomas's *Religion and the Decline of Magic*
Thucydides's *The History of the Peloponnesian War*
Frederick Jackson Turner's *The Significance of the Frontier in American History*
Odd Arne Westad's *The Global Cold War: Third World Interventions And The Making Of Our Times*

LITERATURE

Chinua Achebe's *An Image of Africa: Racism in Conrad's Heart of Darkness*
Roland Barthes's *Mythologies*
Homi K. Bhabha's *The Location of Culture*
Judith Butler's *Gender Trouble*
Simone De Beauvoir's *The Second Sex*
Ferdinand De Saussure's *Course in General Linguistics*
T. S. Eliot's *The Sacred Wood: Essays on Poetry and Criticism*
Zora Neale Huston's *Characteristics of Negro Expression*
Toni Morrison's *Playing in the Dark: Whiteness in the American Literary Imagination*
Edward Said's *Orientalism*
Gayatri Chakravorty Spivak's *Can the Subaltern Speak?*
Mary Wollstonecraft's *A Vindication of the Rights of Women*
Virginia Woolf's *A Room of One's Own*

PHILOSOPHY

Elizabeth Anscombe's *Modern Moral Philosophy*
Hannah Arendt's *The Human Condition*
Aristotle's *Metaphysics*
Aristotle's *Nicomachean Ethics*
Edmund Gettier's *Is Justified True Belief Knowledge?*
Georg Wilhelm Friedrich Hegel's *Phenomenology of Spirit*
David Hume's *Dialogues Concerning Natural Religion*
David Hume's *The Enquiry for Human Understanding*
Immanuel Kant's *Religion within the Boundaries of Mere Reason*
Immanuel Kant's *Critique of Pure Reason*
Søren Kierkegaard's *The Sickness Unto Death*
Søren Kierkegaard's *Fear and Trembling*
C. S. Lewis's *The Abolition of Man*
Alasdair MacIntyre's *After Virtue*
Marcus Aurelius's *Meditations*
Friedrich Nietzsche's *On the Genealogy of Morality*
Friedrich Nietzsche's *Beyond Good and Evil*
Plato's *Republic*
Plato's *Symposium*
Jean-Jacques Rousseau's *The Social Contract*
Gilbert Ryle's *The Concept of Mind*
Baruch Spinoza's *Ethics*
Sun Tzu's *The Art of War*
Ludwig Wittgenstein's *Philosophical Investigations*

POLITICS

Benedict Anderson's *Imagined Communities*
Aristotle's *Politics*
Bernard Bailyn's *The Ideological Origins of the American Revolution*
Edmund Burke's *Reflections on the Revolution in France*
John C. Calhoun's *A Disquisition on Government*
Ha-Joon Chang's *Kicking Away the Ladder*
Hamid Dabashi's *Iran: A People Interrupted*
Hamid Dabashi's *Theology of Discontent: The Ideological Foundation of the Islamic Revolution in Iran*
Robert Dahl's *Democracy and its Critics*
Robert Dahl's *Who Governs?*
David Brion Davis's *The Problem of Slavery in the Age of Revolution*

The Macat Library By Discipline

Alexis De Tocqueville's *Democracy in America*
James Ferguson's *The Anti-Politics Machine*
Frank Dikotter's *Mao's Great Famine*
Sheila Fitzpatrick's *Everyday Stalinism*
Eric Foner's *Reconstruction: America's Unfinished Revolution, 1863-1877*
Milton Friedman's *Capitalism and Freedom*
Francis Fukuyama's *The End of History and the Last Man*
John Lewis Gaddis's *We Now Know: Rethinking Cold War History*
Ernest Gellner's *Nations and Nationalism*
David Graeber's *Debt: the First 5000 Years*
Antonio Gramsci's *The Prison Notebooks*
Alexander Hamilton, John Jay & James Madison's *The Federalist Papers*
Friedrich Hayek's *The Road to Serfdom*
Christopher Hill's *The World Turned Upside Down*
Thomas Hobbes's *Leviathan*
John A. Hobson's *Imperialism: A Study*
Samuel P. Huntington's *The Clash of Civilizations and the Remaking of World Order*
Tony Judt's *Postwar: A History of Europe Since 1945*
David C. Kang's *China Rising: Peace, Power and Order in East Asia*
Paul Kennedy's *The Rise and Fall of Great Powers*
Robert Keohane's *After Hegemony*
Martin Luther King Jr.'s *Why We Can't Wait*
Henry Kissinger's *World Order: Reflections on the Character of Nations and the Course of History*
John Locke's *Two Treatises of Government*
Niccolò Machiavelli's *The Prince*
Thomas Robert Malthus's *An Essay on the Principle of Population*
Mahmood Mamdani's *Citizen and Subject: Contemporary Africa And The Legacy Of Late Colonialism*
Karl Marx's *Capital*
John Stuart Mill's *On Liberty*
John Stuart Mill's *Utilitarianism*
Hans Morgenthau's *Politics Among Nations*
Thomas Paine's *Common Sense*
Thomas Paine's *Rights of Man*
Thomas Piketty's *Capital in the Twenty-First Century*
Robert D. Putman's *Bowling Alone*
John Rawls's *Theory of Justice*
Jean-Jacques Rousseau's *The Social Contract*
Theda Skocpol's *States and Social Revolutions*
Adam Smith's *The Wealth of Nations*
Sun Tzu's *The Art of War*
Henry David Thoreau's *Civil Disobedience*
Thucydides's *The History of the Peloponnesian War*
Kenneth Waltz's *Theory of International Politics*
Max Weber's *Politics as a Vocation*
Odd Arne Westad's *The Global Cold War: Third World Interventions And The Making Of Our Times*

POSTCOLONIAL STUDIES

Roland Barthes's *Mythologies*
Frantz Fanon's *Black Skin, White Masks*
Homi K. Bhabha's *The Location of Culture*
Gustavo Gutiérrez's *A Theology of Liberation*
Edward Said's *Orientalism*
Gayatri Chakravorty Spivak's *Can the Subaltern Speak?*

PSYCHOLOGY

Gordon Allport's *The Nature of Prejudice*
Alan Baddeley & Graham Hitch's *Aggression: A Social Learning Analysis*
Albert Bandura's *Aggression: A Social Learning Analysis*
Leon Festinger's *A Theory of Cognitive Dissonance*
Sigmund Freud's *The Interpretation of Dreams*
Betty Friedan's *The Feminine Mystique*
Michael R. Gottfredson & Travis Hirschi's *A General Theory of Crime*
Eric Hoffer's *The True Believer: Thoughts on the Nature of Mass Movements*
William James's *Principles of Psychology*
Elizabeth Loftus's *Eyewitness Testimony*
A. H. Maslow's *A Theory of Human Motivation*
Stanley Milgram's *Obedience to Authority*
Steven Pinker's *The Better Angels of Our Nature*
Oliver Sacks's *The Man Who Mistook His Wife For a Hat*
Richard Thaler & Cass Sunstein's *Nudge: Improving Decisions About Health, Wealth and Happiness*
Amos Tversky's *Judgment under Uncertainty: Heuristics and Biases*
Philip Zimbardo's *The Lucifer Effect*

SCIENCE

Rachel Carson's *Silent Spring*
William Cronon's *Nature's Metropolis: Chicago And The Great West*
Alfred W. Crosby's *The Columbian Exchange*
Charles Darwin's *On the Origin of Species*
Richard Dawkin's *The Selfish Gene*
Thomas Kuhn's *The Structure of Scientific Revolutions*
Geoffrey Parker's *Global Crisis: War, Climate Change and Catastrophe in the Seventeenth Century*
Mathis Wackernagel & William Rees's *Our Ecological Footprint*

SOCIOLOGY

Michelle Alexander's *The New Jim Crow: Mass Incarceration in the Age of Colorblindness*
Gordon Allport's *The Nature of Prejudice*
Albert Bandura's *Aggression: A Social Learning Analysis*
Hanna Batatu's *The Old Social Classes And The Revolutionary Movements Of Iraq*
Ha-Joon Chang's *Kicking Away the Ladder*
W. E. B. Du Bois's *The Souls of Black Folk*
Émile Durkheim's *On Suicide*
Frantz Fanon's *Black Skin, White Masks*
Frantz Fanon's *The Wretched of the Earth*
Eric Foner's *Reconstruction: America's Unfinished Revolution, 1863-1877*
Eugene Genovese's *Roll, Jordan, Roll: The World the Slaves Made*
Jack Goldstone's *Revolution and Rebellion in the Early Modern World*
Antonio Gramsci's *The Prison Notebooks*
Richard Herrnstein & Charles A Murray's *The Bell Curve: Intelligence and Class Structure in American Life*
Eric Hoffer's *The True Believer: Thoughts on the Nature of Mass Movements*
Jane Jacobs's *The Death and Life of Great American Cities*
Robert Lucas's *Why Doesn't Capital Flow from Rich to Poor Countries?*
Jay Macleod's *Ain't No Makin' It: Aspirations and Attainment in a Low Income Neighborhood*
Elaine May's *Homeward Bound: American Families in the Cold War Era*
Douglas McGregor's *The Human Side of Enterprise*
C. Wright Mills's *The Sociological Imagination*

Thomas Piketty's *Capital in the Twenty-First Century*
Robert D. Putman's *Bowling Alone*
David Riesman's *The Lonely Crowd: A Study of the Changing American Character*
Edward Said's *Orientalism*
Joan Wallach Scott's *Gender and the Politics of History*
Theda Skocpol's *States and Social Revolutions*
Max Weber's *The Protestant Ethic and the Spirit of Capitalism*

THEOLOGY

Augustine's *Confessions*
Benedict's *Rule of St Benedict*
Gustavo Gutiérrez's *A Theology of Liberation*
Carole Hillenbrand's *The Crusades: Islamic Perspectives*
David Hume's *Dialogues Concerning Natural Religion*
Immanuel Kant's *Religion within the Boundaries of Mere Reason*
Ernst Kantorowicz's *The King's Two Bodies: A Study in Medieval Political Theology*
Søren Kierkegaard's *The Sickness Unto Death*
C. S. Lewis's *The Abolition of Man*
Saba Mahmood's *The Politics of Piety: The Islamic Revival and the Feminist Subject*
Baruch Spinoza's *Ethics*
Keith Thomas's *Religion and the Decline of Magic*

COMING SOON

Chris Argyris's *The Individual and the Organisation*
Seyla Benhabib's *The Rights of Others*
Walter Benjamin's *The Work Of Art in the Age of Mechanical Reproduction*
John Berger's *Ways of Seeing*
Pierre Bourdieu's *Outline of a Theory of Practice*
Mary Douglas's *Purity and Danger*
Roland Dworkin's *Taking Rights Seriously*
James G. March's *Exploration and Exploitation in Organisational Learning*
Ikujiro Nonaka's *A Dynamic Theory of Organizational Knowledge Creation*
Griselda Pollock's *Vision and Difference*
Amartya Sen's *Inequality Re-Examined*
Susan Sontag's *On Photography*
Yasser Tabbaa's *The Transformation of Islamic Art*
Ludwig von Mises's *Theory of Money and Credit*

Macat Disciplines

Access the greatest ideas and thinkers across entire disciplines, including

THE FUTURE OF DEMOCRACY

Robert A. Dahl's, *Democracy and Its Critics*
Robert A. Dahl's, *Who Governs?*
Alexis De Toqueville's, *Democracy in America*
Niccolò Machiavelli's, *The Prince*
John Stuart Mill's, *On Liberty*
Robert D. Putnam's, *Bowling Alone*
Jean-Jacques Rousseau's, *The Social Contract*
Henry David Thoreau's, *Civil Disobedience*

Macat analyses are available from all good bookshops and libraries.

Access hundreds of analyses through one, multimedia tool.
Join free for one month **library.macat.com**

Printed in the United States
by Baker & Taylor Publisher Services

Printed in the United States
by Baker & Taylor Publisher Services